CYCLING LÔN LAS CYMRU

About the Author

After years of road running and mountaineering had wreaked havoc with his knees, Richard Barrett returned to long-distance cycling in his fifties when he bought himself a classic British-made touring bike. Now in his sixties, he rides a hand-made bike from one of the great British frame makers that have appeared in recent years. Combined with walking, cycling allows him to continue his love affair with the more mountainous parts of the UK which he first visited as a teenager.

He spent his career in marketing in a number of multinational organisations in the UK and abroad, but he now lives in West Cheshire and rides two or three times a week with groups on both sides of the border.

Other Cicerone guides by the author
Cycling in the Hebrides
Cycling in the Lake District
The Hebridean Way
Walking on Harris and Lewis

CYCLING LÔN LAS CYMRU

250 MILES THROUGH THE HEART OF WALES
ON TRAFFIC-FREE PATHS AND QUIET ROADS

by Richard Barrett

JUNIPER HOUSE, MURLEY MOSS,
OXENHOLME ROAD, KENDAL, CUMBRIA LA9 7RL
www.cicerone.co.uk

© Richard Barrett 2018
First edition 2018
ISBN: 978 1 85284 987 0

Printed in China on behalf of Latitude Press Ltd.
A catalogue record for this book is available from the British Library.
All photographs are by the author unless otherwise stated.

Route mapping by Lovell Johns www.lovelljohns.com
© Crown copyright 2018 OS PU100012932.
NASA relief data courtesy of ESRI

Dedication

*This book is dedicated to those stalwarts who lobby for better facilities for cyclists
and give up their time to maintain Sustrans routes in their neighbourhood.*

Acknowledgements

My thanks to Jonathan and Joe Williams of Cicerone for commissioning this book
and in so doing introducing me to wonderful bits of the country I had never
previously visited. I should also like to thank Sian, Verity, Stephanie and the
production team, who once again made the process such a pleasure.

Updates to this Guide

While every effort is made by our authors to ensure the accuracy of guidebooks as
they go to print, changes can occur during the lifetime of an edition. Any updates
that we know of for this guide will be on the Cicerone website (www.cicerone.
co.uk/987/updates), so please check before planning your trip. We also advise
that you check information about such things as transport, accommodation and
shops locally. Even rights of way can be altered over time. We are always grateful
for information about any discrepancies between a guidebook and the facts on
the ground, sent by email to updates@cicerone.co.uk or by post to Cicerone,
Juniper House, Murley Moss, Oxenholme Road, Kendal, LA9 7RL.

   Register your book: To sign up to receive free updates, special offers and
GPX files where available, register your book at www.cicerone.co.uk.

Front cover: Parked up at my preferred ending – South Stack Lighthouse (Stage 5)

CONTENTS

GPX files

GPX files for all routes can be downloaded free at www.cicerone.co.uk/987/GPX.

Route maps are at a scale of 1:200,000. All other maps, including town maps, vary. Please refer to the scale on the map.

ROUTE SUMMARY TABLE

Stage	Start	End	Distance (miles/km)	Ascent (m)	Time (hrs at 10mph/ 16kph + 400m/hr)	Page
1	Cardiff	Glasbury	70/112	1200	10–11	32
1a (Alt start)	Chepstow	Glasbury	57/91	1500	9–10	49
2	Glasbury	Llanidloes	48/77	1000	7–8	64
3	Llanidloes	Dolgellau	39/62	1200	7–8	74
4	Dolgellau	Caernarfon	60/96	1100	9–10	84
5	Caernarfon	Holyhead	38/61	500	5–6	103
Total			**255/408**	**5000**	**38–43**	
Total (Alt start)			**242/387**	**5300**	**37–42**	

The Brecon Beacons from the north (Stage 1)

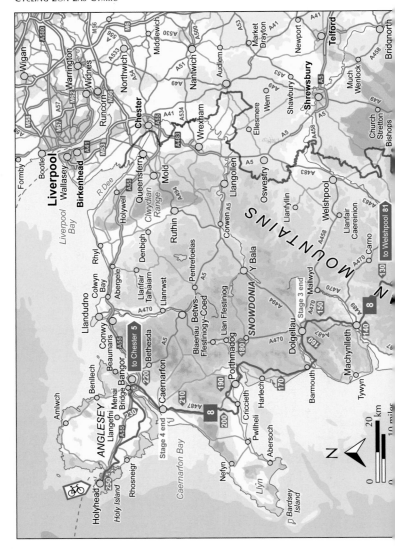

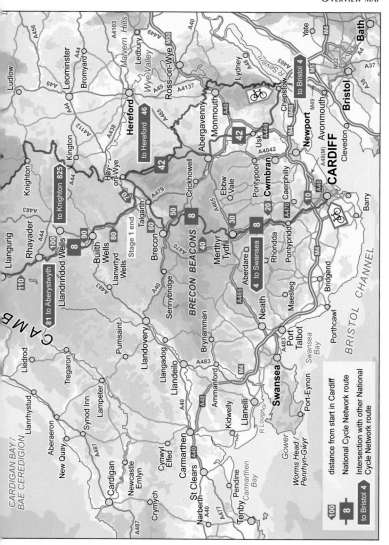

Ride planner from Cardiff

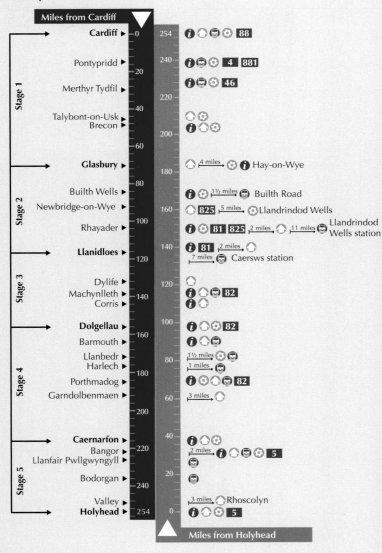

Miles from Cardiff

	Miles from Cardiff	
Cardiff ▶	0 / 254	ℹ️ 🏠 🚉 ⚙️ **88**
Pontypridd ▶	20 / 240	ℹ️ 🚉 ⚙️ **4** **881**
Merthyr Tydfil ▶	/	ℹ️ 🚉 ⚙️ **46**
	40 / 220	
Talybont-on-Usk ▶	/	🏠 ⚙️
Brecon ▶	/ 200	ℹ️ 🏠 ⚙️
	60 /	
Glasbury ▶	/ 180	🏠 →4 miles→ ⚙️ ℹ️ Hay-on-Wye
	80 /	
Builth Wells ▶	/	ℹ️ ⚙️ →1½ miles→ 🚉 Builth Road
Newbridge-on-Wye ▶	/ 160	🏠 **825** →5 miles→ ⚙️ Llandrindod Wells
Rhayader ▶	100 /	ℹ️ ⚙️ **81** **825** →2 miles→ 🏠 →11 miles→ 🚉 Llandrindod Wells station
Llanidloes ▶	120 / 140	ℹ️ **81** →2 miles→ 🏠
	/	→7 miles→ 🚉 Caersws station
Dylife ▶	/ 120	🏠
Machynlleth ▶	140 /	ℹ️ 🏠 🚉 **82**
Corris ▶	/	ℹ️ 🏠
Dolgellau ▶	160 / 100	ℹ️ 🏠 ⚙️ **82**
Barmouth ▶	/	ℹ️ 🏠 🚉
Llanbedr ▶	/ 80	→1½ miles→ ⚙️ 🚉
Harlech ▶	180 /	→1 miles→ 🚉
Porthmadog ▶	/	ℹ️ ⚙️ 🏠 🚉 **82**
Garndolbenmaen ▶	200 / 60	→3 miles→ 🏠
Caernarfon ▶	40 /	ℹ️ 🏠 ⚙️
Bangor ▶	220 /	→2 miles→ ℹ️ 🏠 🚉 ⚙️ **5**
Llanfair Pwllgwyngyll ▶	/	🚉
Bodorgan ▶	/ 20	🚉
Valley ▶	240 /	→3 miles→ 🏠 Rhoscolyn
Holyhead ▶	254 / 0	ℹ️ 🏠 ⚙️ **5**

Miles from Holyhead

Stage 1 · Stage 2 · Stage 3 · Stage 4 · Stage 5

ℹ️ Tourist information 🏠 Hostel 🚉 Rail station ⚙️ Cycle shop **88** NCR link

Ride planner from Chepstow

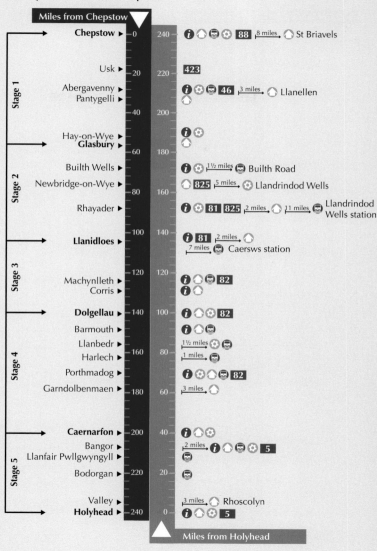

Miles from Chepstow

		Miles from Chepstow		
Stage 1	Chepstow ▶	0 — 240	ℹ️ 🏠 🚆 ⚙️ **88** ⎯8 miles⎯ 🏠 St Briavels
	Usk ▶	20 — 220	**423**
	Abergavenny ▶ Pantygelli ▶	— 200 40	ℹ️ 🚆 ⚙️ **46** ⎯3 miles⎯ 🏠 Llanellen 🏠
Stage 2	Hay-on-Wye ▶ **Glasbury** ▶	60 — 180	ℹ️ ⚙️ 🏠
	Builth Wells ▶		ℹ️ ⚙️ ⎯1½ miles⎯ 🚆 Builth Road
	Newbridge-on-Wye ▶	— 160 80	🏠 **825** ⎯5 miles⎯ ⚙️ Llandrindod Wells
	Rhayader ▶		ℹ️ ⚙️ **81** **825** ⎯2 miles⎯ 🏠 ⎯11 miles⎯ 🚆 Llandrindod Wells station
Stage 3	**Llanidloes** ▶	100 — 140	ℹ️ **81** ⎯2 miles⎯ 🏠 ⎯7 miles⎯ 🚆 Caersws station
	Machynlleth ▶ Corris ▶	120 — 120	ℹ️ 🏠 🚆 **82** ℹ️ 🏠
Stage 4	**Dolgellau** ▶	140 — 100	ℹ️ 🏠 ⚙️ **82**
	Barmouth ▶		ℹ️ 🏠 🚆
	Llanbedr ▶	— 80 160	⎯1½ miles⎯ ⚙️ 🚆
	Harlech ▶		⎯1 miles⎯ 🚆
	Porthmadog ▶		ℹ️ ⚙️ 🏠 🚆 **82**
	Garndolbenmaen ▶	180 — 60	⎯3 miles⎯ 🏠
Stage 5	**Caernarfon** ▶	200 — 40	ℹ️ 🏠 ⚙️
	Bangor ▶ Llanfair Pwllgwyngyll ▶		⎯2 miles⎯ ℹ️ 🏠 🚆 ⚙️ **5** 🚆
	Bodorgan ▶	220 — 20	🚆
	Valley ▶		⎯3 miles⎯ 🏠 Rhoscolyn
	Holyhead ▶	240 — 0	ℹ️ 🏠 ⚙️ **5**

Miles from Holyhead

ℹ️ Tourist information   🏠 Hostel   🚆 Rail station   ⚙️ Cycle shop   **88** NCR link

Suggested schedule summary from Cardiff

Miles from Cardiff ▼	4 DAYS	5 DAYS	6 DAYS	7 DAYS
Cardiff ► 0			**Cardiff to Talybon-on-Usk** *49 miles 6–7hr 800m ascent*	**Cardiff to Talybont-on-Usk** *49 miles 6–7hr 800m ascent*
Pontypridd ► 20	**Cardiff to Glasbury** *70 miles 10–11hr 1200m ascent*	**Cardiff to Glasbury** *70 miles 10–11hr 1200m ascent*		
Merthyr Tydfil ►				
40				
Talybont-on-Usk ►			**Talybont on Usk to Newbridge-on-Wye** *43 miles 6–7hr 700m ascent*	**Talybont on Usk to Builth Wells** *37 miles 5–6hr 700m ascent*
Brecon ►				
60				
Glasbury ►				
80	**Glasbury to Llandiloes** *48 miles 7–8hr 1000m ascent*	**Glasbury to Llandiloes** *48 miles 7–8hr 1000m ascent*		**Builth Wells to Llandiloes** *31 miles 5–6hr 800m ascent*
Builth Wells ►				
Newbridge-on-Wye ►			**Newbridge-on-Wye to Machynlleth** *47 miles 7–8hr 1200m ascent*	
Rhayader ► 100				
Llanidloes ► 120				**Llanidloes to Dolgellau** *39 miles 7–8hr 1200m ascent*
Dylife ►	**Llandiloes to Harlech** *59 miles 10–11hr 1600m ascent*	**Llandiloes to Dolgellau** *39 miles 7–8hr 1200m ascent*		
Machynlleth ► 140			**Machynlleth to Harlech** *37 miles 6–7hr 1100m ascent*	
Corris ►				
Dolgellau ► 160		**Dolgellau to Caernarfon** *60 miles 9–10hr 1300m ascent*		**Dolgellau to Porthmadog** *33 miles 5–6hr 800m ascent*
Barmouth ►				
Llanbedr ►			**Harlech to Caernarfon** *41 miles 6–7hr 900m ascent*	
Harlech ► 180				
Porthmadog ►				**Portmadog to Caernarfon** *28 miles 3–4hr 400m ascent*
Garndolbenmaen ► 200	**Harlech to Holyhead** *78 miles 11–12hr 1400m ascent*			
Caernarfon ► 220		**Caernarfon to Holyhead** *38 miles 5–6hr 500m ascent*	**Caernarfon to Holyhead** *38 miles 5–6hr 500m ascent*	**Caernarfon to Holyhead** *38 miles 5–6hr 500m ascent*
Bangor ►				
Llanfair Pwllgwyngyll ►				
Bodorgan ► 240				
Valley ►				
Holyhead ► 254				

Suggested schedule summary from Chepstow

Miles from Chepstow	4 DAYS	5 DAYS	6 DAYS	7 DAYS
Chepstow ► 0				Chepstow to Abergavenny *30 miles 5–6hr 800m ascent*
Usk ► 20	Chepstow to Glasbury *57 miles 9–10hr 1500m ascent*	Chepstow to Glasbury *57 miles 9–10hr 1500m ascent*	Chepstow to Hay-on-Wye *52 miles 8–9hr 1400m ascent*	
Abergavenny ► Pantgelli ► 40				Abergavenny to Newbridge-on-Wye *50 miles 7–8hr 1100m ascent*
Hay-on-Wye ► Glasbury ► 60			Hay-on-Wye to Rhayader *38 miles 6–7hr 800m ascent*	
Builth Wells ►	Glasbury to Machynlleth *71 miles 11–12hr 1600m ascent*	Glasbury to Llandiloes *48 miles 7–8hr 1000m ascent*		Newbridge-on-Wye to Llandiloes *24 miles 4–5hr 700m ascent*
Newbridge-on-Wye ► 80			Rhayader to Corris *44 miles 7–8hr 1100m ascent*	
Rhayader ►				Llandiloes to Dolgellau *39 miles 7–8hr 1200m ascent*
Llanidloes ► 100		Llandiloes to Dolgellau *39 miles 7–8hr 1200m ascent*		
120				
Machynlleth ► Corris ►	Machynlleth to Porthmadog *47 miles 8–9hr 1400m ascent*		Corris to Porthmadog *41 miles 7–8hr 1200m ascent*	Dolgellau to Porthmadog *33 miles 5–6hr 800m ascent*
Dolgellau ► 140				
Barmouth ►		Dolgellau to Caernarfon *60 miles 9–10hr 1300m ascent*		
Llanbedr ► 160				
Harlech ►				
Porthmadog ►			Porthmadog to Caernarfon *29 miles 4–5hr 500m ascent*	Portmadog to Caernarfon *28 miles 3–4hr 400m ascent*
Garndolbenmaen ► 180				
200 Caernarfon ►	Porthmadog to Holyhead *67 miles 9–10hr 1000m ascent*			
Bangor ►		Caernarfon to Holyhead *38 miles 5–6hr 500m ascent*	Caernarfon to Holyhead *38 miles 5–6hr 500m ascent*	Caernarfon to Holyhead *38 miles 5–6hr 500m ascent*
Llanfair Pwllgwyngyll ►				
Bodorgan ► 220				
Valley ►				
Holyhead ► 240				

13

Ornate gate in Llansantffraed-Cwmdeuddwr at the start of the Elan Valley cycleway which is briefly shared by Lôn Las Cymru (Stage 2)

INTRODUCTION

Looking north along Talybont Reservoir (Stage 1)

Lôn Las Cymru runs from Cardiff or Chepstow to Holyhead, passing through the heart of Wales. Translating loosely as Wales' Green Lane, it is the preeminent cycle route in Wales, passing through lush countryside, and following quiet lanes and former railway lines.

The route from Cardiff is just over 250 miles (400km) or, from the alternative start in Chepstow, it is just over 240 miles (390km). It passes through the Brecon Beacons National Park and Snowdonia National Park and over the Black Mountains, the Brecon Beacons, and the Cambrian Mountains of Mid Wales taking in some of the most stunning and diverse landscapes in the British Isles.

Crossing the mountains requires a good level of fitness but should not trouble the average rider on an average bike as the gradients are mostly gentle. The panoramic views from the top of the Gospel Pass, Bryn Y Fedwen and Moel Goedog make the climbs worth the effort too. The scenery on the flatter sections is equally stunning, especially up Wye Valley and along the quiet lanes on Anglesey.

Travelling through such wonderful countryside by bike is hugely satisfying both for those who want to cover the miles quickly and those preferring a more leisurely pace to watch wildlife and explore attractions along the way. There are plenty of pretty villages and interesting towns where you can

The magnificent red kite is a common sight in the Cambrian Mountains (Image authorised for common usage)

top up the energy levels in local cafés and interesting shops where you can replenish supplies. These towns also provide a good choice of overnight accommodation and places for dinner, although you may need to leave the route to find exactly what you're looking for. Add to that an impressive collection of castles, industrial archaeology, churches, chapels and prehistoric sites along the route – and the red kites and common buzzards that are frequently soaring overhead – and you have a ride that you will remember for a very long time.

The cycle charity, Sustrans, designed the route to take in minor roads and avoid busy parts of towns and cities by using traffic-free paths along rivers and dismantled railways. From Cardiff, it follows the Taff Trail to Brecon with the first 34 miles being entirely traffic-free before climbing the gap between the Brecon Beacons and the Black Mountains. The route from the alternative start at Chepstow is less urban, passing those market towns of Usk and Abergavenny and over the magnificent Gospel Pass before dropping down to the literary town of Hay-on-Wye.

After coming together near Glasbury, the route follows the Wye Valley and then the upper reaches of the River Seven before two mountainous stretches first through the Cambrian Mountains, then through the hills near Cader Idris. There is plenty of time to recover along the Mawddach Trail and the promenade at Barmouth before the route turns inland to climb across the hills above Harlech. After that, with most of the hard work done, it is pleasant riding through the tourist resorts along Tremadog Bay, before crossing the low-lying Llŷn Peninsula. There is more easy riding along Lôn Eifion and Lôn Las Menai to the Menai Bridge. Once on Anglesey, it is easy riding all the way to the end at Holyhead – or with just a little extra effort you can opt for a more spectacular finish at South Stack Lighthouse.

DR BEECHING: THE UNKNOWING ENABLER OF LÔN LAS CYMRU

In addition to the staff of Sustrans and the various county councils along the route, we should posthumously thank Richard Beeching (1913–1985) for his unwitting help in the creation of Lôn Las Cymru. A brilliant physicist and engineer who held senior positions in both industry and the civil service, in 1961 Beeching was controversially appointed as the first Chairman of the newly created British Railways Board commissioned with curtailing growing losses and returning the industry to profitability.

He recommended closing one-third of the country's 7000 railway stations and 5000 miles of track resulting in the loss of 70,000 jobs. Unsurprisingly, such proposals were hugely controversial and many were rejected by the government, which terminated Beeching's contract early allowing him to return to industry. Protests resulted in some stations and lines being saved, but eventually the majority were closed as planned.

Over the years, some routes reopened including a few in the Welsh Valleys. Other sections have been preserved as Heritage Railways or turned into roads. But some rural and urban lines have been absorbed into the National Cycle Network to give hundreds of miles of traffic-free cycling. Lôn Las Cymru includes the following stretches of shared-use paths which follow the route of former railway lines: the Taff Trail (55 miles), the Mawddach Trail (9½ miles), Lôn Eifion (12½ miles) and Lôn Las Menai (4 miles). In total that is 81 miles of traffic-free cycling that became possible because of the 'Beeching Axe'.

WHY LÔN LAS CYMRU?

Lôn Las Cymru crosses from the industrial south to the sea cliffs of Anglesey passing through wild mountains and along green valleys where some of the events that shaped Wales took place. Singing may come automatically as each new vista unfolds. In addition to the beautiful, varied landscape, there is a great satisfaction in doing a ride that crosses the entire length of a country, and covers its industrial heritage and its remote and sparsely-populated heartland.

With over 80 miles of traffic-free, shared-use paths and the rest following quiet lanes, Lôn Las Cymru is also the ideal tour for anyone averse to busy roads. In fact it follows such quiet roads through towns that you will inevitably find yourself straying off route to find lunch.

Route finding is simple and the start and finish points are all easily accessible by train. So too are many locations along the way so you can easily ride the route over a couple of short breaks rather than one holiday.

Looking north from the top of the Gospel Pass (Stage 1a)

HOW TOUGH IS IT?

Lôn Las Cymru can be ridden as a leisure activity or as a challenge and this guidebook has schedules for both types of rider. There are some mountainous sections in Mid Wales. However, gradients are never severe and some, such as that up the Vale of Ewyas, barely perceptible until the very top.

WHICH DIRECTION TO RIDE?

Because of the prevailing southwesterly winds, it is usually easier to ride Lôn Las Cymru from south to north as described in this guidebook. Riding in that direction also means you are not riding into the sun and quickly escape the urban landscape. However if you have an emotional attachment with South Wales, you may want to ride the route in the opposite direction. There is some guidance to help you in the North to South boxes at the end of each stage, but you will need to adapt the directions in the route descriptions.

SELECTING A SCHEDULE

The five stages of this book are meant as a guide and may not coincide with your personal itinerary: that will depend on the time you have available, your daily mileage and whether you visit attractions along the way. Please see the front of the guide for a summary of suggested schedules, starting from both Cardiff and Chepstow. As a general guide, if you want a more relaxed schedule allow more time for the central mountainous section of the route.

The availability of accommodation will also determine where your days begin and end, which could be at places before the end of a stage, into the following stage or perhaps somewhere off the route altogether. When planning your ride:

- First decide how many days you can spare or need.
- Use the suggested schedules at the beginning of the guide to identify roughly where each day will ideally begin and end.

- Identify the most convenient accommodation that suits your budget around the chosen start and finish points. This may mean amending your initial schedule so be prepared to be flexible, perhaps enjoying a night in a B&B if there are no hostels nearby and vice versa.
- Book your accommodation and finalise your schedule. You will have more choice about where to stay if you book well in advance of your departure date.

GETTING THERE

Many local cyclists will happily add an extra day or two to either end of their tour and make use of the National Cycle Network to return to the start point on their bike. But others from further afield and those pressed for time will undoubtedly need another form of transport.

If you are riding as a group you may be able to commandeer someone to drop you at one end and collect you from the other. Some lucky groups may have their support vehicle stay with them to move luggage between stops and provide catering support.

If you are not riding in a big group or on a tandem, the easiest way to access the route is by train as Cardiff, Chepstow and Holyhead are all on the national rail network. Similarly, there are a number of stations along the route so you can easily split the ride into sections. See 'By rail' below for further details.

For details on all public transport journeys throughout the UK,

All correctly ticketed awaiting the morning train

Rail stations on or adjacent to Lôn Las Cymru

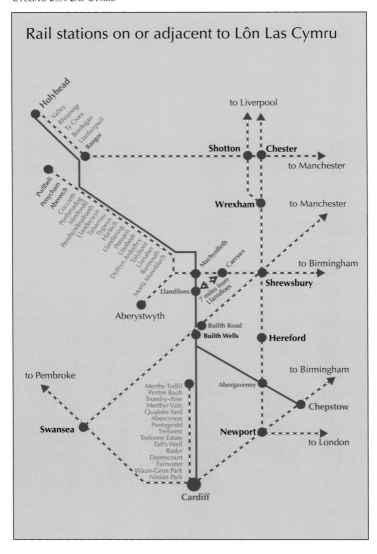

including local bus services, call Traveline on 0871 200 2233 or visit www.traveline.info or www.traveline.cymru. See also Appendix C for a list of transport providers and their contact details.

By rail

There are numerous ways to access Lôn Las Cymru by train, as detailed in the notes below, but for general information on travel by rail call 08457 484 950 or visit www.nationalrail.co.uk.

Cardiff station near the start or finish of Lôn Las Cymru provides direct trains to most parts of the UK. Great Western Railway provide services between the south of England and Cardiff. They have space for bicycles on most trains but ask that you can reserve your bike space when you book your tickets online or at a ticket office or by calling 0345 7000 125. See www.gwr.com for details.

Holyhead station near the start or finish of Lôn Las Cymru is on the North Wales Coast line and provides direct trains via Bangor to Chester and Cardiff with connections to most other parts of the UK. Virgin Trains run mainline services to and from Holyhead. They provide special bike storage areas with space for up to four bikes, but you will need to book a reservation for your bike before you travel. The service is free and can be made at any booking office or by calling 0344 556 5650. On the day of travel, you will need to collect

your bike reservation coupons at a FastTicket machine at the station by keying in your FastTicket reference number and the number of the bank card you used to make the booking. Then give yourself a minimum of 10 minutes to contact a member of the Virgin platform staff who will help you load your bicycle. Once aboard, inform the Train Manager that you have a bicycle and they will help you disembark at your destination station. Sounds complicated, but it seems to work even though local staff may not be entirely familiar with the process. See www.virgintrains.co.uk for details.

Chepstow station near the alternative start or finish of Lôn Las Cymru is on the Newport to Birmingham line with connections to most other parts of the UK. Visit www.arrivatrainswales.co.uk for further details.

Intermediary stations on or near the route are provided by Arriva Trains Wales who provide bike space on all of their services except for some Valleys and Cardiff local routes during peak hours. They recommend that you make a reservation as far in advance as possible and reserve a cycle space at the time of purchasing your ticket. You can do this at any staffed national rail station or by calling their telesales office on 0870 9000 773. See www.arrivatrainswales.co.uk for further details.

- Abergavenny station is on the Newport to Hereford line.

- Builth Road station, which is 1½ miles outside of Builth Wells, is on the Shrewsbury to Swansea line.
- Llandrindod Wells station is just over 5 miles from Newbridge-on-Wye on the National Cycle Route 825.
- Caersws station, 7 miles to the northeast of Llanidloes on National Cycle Route 81, is on the Aberystwyth to Shrewsbury line with direct services through to Birmingham and beyond.
- Barmouth, Criccieth, Porthmadog, Harlech and other stations on the Cambrian Coast line are close to Lôn Las Cymru and provide services via Machynlleth to Shrewsbury and Birmingham with connections to most other parts of the UK.

By bus

National Express, Britain's only scheduled coach network, say they may carry dismantled and folding bicycles if space is available provided they are suitably packed. They also state that carrying a bike on a service does not mean that they will carry it on any subsequent service. As this gives cyclists no reassurance that their bike will actually be carried, let alone any advice what to do with the transit box when they want to start cycling, they may as well say, 'No'!

The same goes for the Traws Cambria service between South and North Wales which involves a number of stages each operated by a different bus company. Not all of them carry bikes and you are advised to contact each operator individually. A further deterrent is that the journey takes 11 hours. For further information visit www.trawscymru.info or call 0300 200 2233.

By air

Cardiff airport near the southern end of the route provides international and domestic services. Anglesey airport near the northern end of the route only provides a twice daily service to and from Cardiff. Other airports are Manchester, Liverpool, Birmingham and Bristol although arriving at any one of these airports still leaves you with a journey of 100 miles or more necessitating using public transport or hiring a car.

If you are planning to fly with your bike, you should contact your airline and make a reservation when you book your seat. They will charge you for carrying your bike and will ask that you follow their packing instructions. These typically include turning and locking the handlebars parallel with the frame, removing the pedals and front wheel and attaching them to the frame, and deflating the tyres before placing the bike in a carrying bag or transit box.

By ferry

Stena Line operates between Dublin or Dun Laoghaire and Holyhead. Visit www.stenaline.co.uk or call 0344 847 0008 for details. Irish Ferries operates

Built in 1897 as the headquarters for the Bute Dock Company, the Pierhead Building in Cardiff Bay is now used by the National Assembly for Wales (Stage 1)

between Dublin and Holyhead. Visit www.irishferries.co.uk or call 08717 300 400 for details.

FIRST AND LAST NIGHTS

Cardiff

Cardiff is easily accessible by rail and there is even an extension of NCR8 that runs for 2 miles from the main station to the start of the route in Cardiff Bay. There is also a huge choice of accommodation from five-star hotels to ultra-modern hostels with private rooms and internal bike storage. As Wales's capital city, Cardiff is home to the National Museum, which houses the national art, natural history and geology collections, as well as temporary exhibitions. But there are plenty of other attractions, such as Cardiff Castle and Cardiff Bay, world-famous sporting venues, top class entertainment and quality shopping – making it a great place to spend an extra night.

Chepstow

Getting to Chepstow by train involves a change somewhere in the journey but it may not take longer as the town is right on the border. The town's proximity to the motorway network also makes it easy to get to by car.

It is a pleasant town with plenty of accommodation to suit all pockets. You can visit Chepstow Castle, which was commissioned by William the Conqueror immediately after the Battle of Hastings, making it Britain's oldest surviving post-Roman stone castle, or browse the eclectic range of shops in the handsome Georgian and Victorian town centre. But unless you decide to test out the town's claim that

23

'No better cider does the world supply' expect a fairly quiet night.

Holyhead

Holyhead is a busy ferry port with fast trains that link to the main UK network and plenty of overnight accommodation. But if you ride a few miles to Treaddur and Rhoscolyn you will find plenty more overnight options set in wonderful coastal scenery.

WHEN TO RIDE

The best time to go is between April and October when the days are longer and the weather is at its best. But even then you may experience inclement days so check the weather forecast before you set out so you will know whether to keep your waterproof at the top of your pack and wear your overshoes from the start. But if you are struggling and the weather forecast is atrocious, consider taking the train or seeing whether a local taxi service can move you and your bike along the route. You can always come back and ride the section you missed another time.

ACCOMMODATION

While some cycle tourists prefer to camp, days of repeatedly ascending 1000m or more are unlikely to be pleasurable with heavy luggage. This guide makes maximum use of hostels and bunkhouses along or near the route (see Appendix B for details),

but if you prefer additional comforts you will find a variety of accommodation to suit most pockets on www. visitwales.com – the site of the Welsh Tourist Board. You may not be able to get exactly what you want at the start or finish of each stage so you may have to curtail your day before the end of a stage, ride further into the next stage or temporarily leave the route.

Hostels are always busy during the summer months and those in the more popular locations can be full at weekends and sometimes even in the depths of winter so it pays to book early. The Youth Hostel Association, www.yha.org.uk, has a number of hostels in Wales and there are an increasing number of independent hostels – see www.independenthostelguide. co.uk for details.

It is worth seeking out Visit Wales's star-graded B&Bs, guest houses and hotels enrolled in their 'Cyclists Welcome' scheme which provide drying facilities, bike storage and other services. Whatever you choose, if you want to arrive early to drop off your bike and go sightseeing or anticipate arriving later due to unforeseen delay, it is courteous to ring ahead and let them know.

BAGGAGE TRANSFER

Other than arrange it yourself with local taxi operators, the only easy way to get your luggage transferred each day is to book a self-guided package holiday. See www.droverholidays.co.uk, www.greentraveller.co.uk or www.wheelywonderfulcycling.co.uk.

WHAT TO TAKE

The plethora of accommodation and the high number of cycle shops along the route means you can keep the bike as light as possible. Here are some tips to lighten your load:

- Think layers and add-ons rather than alternatives.
- Rinse through cycling gear and other clothing every evening using drying facilities if available.
- Choose leisurewear, such as long-sleeved T-shirts, that can also be used as an extra layer for chilly days.
- Share tools and accessories.
- Buy travel-sized toiletries and give shaving a miss for the week.
- Make do with a smartphone and leave all other electronics at home.
- Only carry one feed-bottle – it'll be plenty.
- Use accommodation with secure storage and leave the heavy bike lock at home.
- But always wear a helmet as riding without one is irresponsible.

Adopting such guidelines produces the kit list shown in Appendix D, which totals 5–7kg for summer tours and 7–9kg during winter. Having reduced the kit list as much as possible, it should easily fit into a pair of panniers or a set of seat and frame packs.

PREPARING YOUR BIKE

Other than for a very short section on the old coach road between

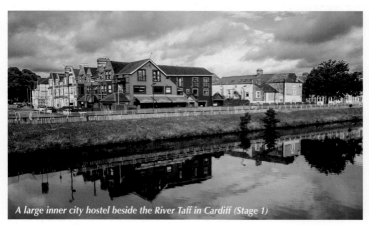

A large inner city hostel beside the River Taff in Cardiff (Stage 1)

Loaded with panniers, heading down the Gospel Pass towards Hay-on-Wye (Stage 1a)

Newbridge-on-Wye and Rhayader, the surface is remarkably good so you can ride the route on a road bike, a mountain bike or a hybrid/city bike. However, there are some things that you can do to make your ride more comfortable:

- Leave your best carbon frame and carbon wheels at home.
- Use tyres that are 28mm or wider as they will be more comfortable.
- Swap mountain bike tyres for lower profile urban tyres which take less effort and give a quieter ride.
- Fit a cassette with a 30, 32 or 34 tooth sprocket to make it easier to climb up hills.
- Fit bar ends to straight handlebars so you have more choice for resting tired hands.
- Attach a bell, which is essential for negotiating pedestrians on shared-use paths.

Whatever you choose, it is always advisable to have your bike serviced a couple of weeks before your trip, allowing sufficient time for any worn parts to be replaced and run-in before your departure. There are plenty of cycle shops en route, see Appendix A for details.

CYCLING DOS AND DON'TS

- Be considerate to others on shared-use paths particularly children and dogs, both can often behave unpredictably. Ring your bell or call out to pass – and always say thank you.
- Although you can legally ride two abreast, quickly move into single file on minor roads always giving a cheery wave to thank considerate drivers.

- Scan ahead for hazards such as road furniture, grit and livestock detritus.
- Avoid the green mossy strip along the centre of tree-lined roads as it may be slippery.
- Always park your bike in a prominent position and secure it with a lock when you go exploring.
- Ride across cattle grids square-on, standing on the pedals with your knees bent, and you will hardly notice them.
- Always use hand signals to make your intentions clear to others.

EATING

Cycling is strenuous so keep your energy reserves topped up by eating frequently otherwise you will soon 'hit the wall' and feel tired and demotivated. However, it is best to avoid a full breakfast as it will weigh heavy for most of the morning. Get into the routine of eating little and often rather than waiting until you feel hungry, as by then it is frequently too late.

Many cyclists rely on things such as sandwiches, fruitcake, cereal bars and fruit. That is not to say, you should ignore the region's many inns and cafés, but err on the side of caution and stick to energy-giving snacks and pastries rather than a full midday meal.

A former hardware store, this is now a popular café in Dolgellau (Stage 3)

PHONES AND WI-FI

Although mobile coverage is generally good, phone users in Wales have the least access to 4G networks in the UK so you may not be able to post your photos straight to social media when riding through the Cambrian Mountains. However, many cafés and pubs provide free Wi-Fi access so you should not be offline for too long.

TEN SPECIALITIES TO TRY WHEN IN WALES

- Bara brith (speckled bread) is a Welsh version of tea loaf enriched with dried fruit and mixed spices, usually served sliced and buttered.

- Glamorgan sausage (*selsig morgannwg*), which is traditionally made from Caerphilly cheese, leeks, breadcrumbs and spices, was popular during World War II when meat was in short supply.

- Cawl, often said to be the national dish of Wales, is a broth made from meat with potatoes, swedes, carrots and other seasonal vegetables, such as leeks.

- Thought to have originated in the Welsh Valleys in the 18th century, Welsh rarebit is cheese on toast, sometimes mixed with onions, egg and milk and seasoned with salt and pepper.

- Crempog is a pancake made with flour, buttermilk, eggs, vinegar and salted butter traditionally served on Shrove Tuesday and other days of celebration, such as birthdays.

- By the time you finish the ride you will have seen thousands on the hillsides so why not try Welsh lamb close to where it is reared.

- Look out for the 'oggie' – a D-shaped pasty made with lamb and leeks.

- Welsh cakes are circular cakes spiced with cinnamon and nutmeg and dusted in caster sugar.

- Laverbread (*bara lawr*) is an edible seaweed usually served with toast or alongside bacon and eggs for breakfast.

- Some quality craft beers are produced on or near the route: Brains, Bullmastiff, Crafty Devil and Tiny Rebel (Cardiff); Bragdy Twt Lol (Treforest); Otley (Pontypridd); Lithic (Llangors); Brecon Brewing (Brecon); Waen (Llanidloes); CwrW Cader (Dolgellau) and Purple Moose (Porthmadog).

EMERGENCIES

You may encounter few fellow cyclists along some of the more remote stages in Mid Wales so it pays to be prepared for problems or emergencies. Should you have a good mobile phone signal, you can telephone the emergency services by dialling 999 or 112. However, it is always wise to let someone know your plans particularly across the more remote hills between Machynlleth and Dolgellau.

WAYMARKING

Lôn Las Cymru (National Cycle Network Route 8) is well signed throughout with fingerposts at major junctions and small blue repeater signs along the way. It can occasionally become confusing when signage for local routes (such as the Taff Trail or Lôn Eifion take precedence), when another NCN route briefly follows the same course or signs are hidden behind undergrowth or temporarily misplaced. So it pays to be attentive at junctions checking both as you approach a junction and as you ride away from it to see if there is signage for riders going in the opposite direction.

Having the route downloaded onto a GPS so that you get a beep at every junction is reassuring but not a necessity. However, they also have a nasty habit of losing satellite connection along the extensive tree-lined sections of the route and you may need to carry a power pack to top up the battery while riding.

MAPS

This book is designed to be small enough to carry with you and includes linear maps that are entirely adequate for following the route. However, they do not show much on either side of the route, such as where your overnight accommodation is located, so it is advisable to carry separate maps, such as those in the Ordnance Survey 1:50,000 Landranger Series for such purposes. The information boxes at the start of each stage specify the numbers of the relevant Ordnance Survey map sheets should you wish to explore.

USING THIS GUIDE

Although the guide is organised into five stages, you may wish to choose one of the suggested alternative schedules or work out your own itinerary. Each stage starts and finishes at a location where there is a selection of different types of accommodation and good local facilities. At the beginning of each stage, an information box summarises the practical details associated with the stage, including start and finish points (with grid references), distance, total ascent and the relevant Ordnance Survey map sheets. There is an estimate of the time required to complete the stage, although this will of course vary considerably according to fitness and the prevailing weather. Details of attractions and services along the stage are also provided.

ESTIMATING TIMES IN HILLY TERRAIN

Estimating how long a ride will take when it involves a significant amount of climbing is notoriously difficult. Hillwalkers use Naismith's Rule which allows one hour for every 3 miles covered in distance plus one hour for every 2000ft (600m) of ascent. Because there is considerable variation between the speed and climbing abilities of a committed club cyclist and a leisure cyclist, there is no comparable benchmark in cycling. However, the basic principle still applies:

Total time = time to cover the distance + time spent ascending

The Italian physician and cycling coach Michele Ferrari developed the term *velocità ascensionale media* (VAM) to refer to the average speed of ascent. VAM is usually expressed as metres per hour (m/h) and winners of mountain stages in grand tours typically climb at more than 1500m/h, while most club cyclists are capable of climbing somewhere in the range between 700 and 900m/h.

In this book much more modest values have been used for VAM with estimated times based on 10 mph (16kph) plus 400m/h. So a stage of 50 miles that involves 800m of ascent is estimated to take roughly seven hours.

To get an estimate of your own VAM, first assess your average speed on the flat and then record your times for a number of measured climbs and see what number best fits. But if all of this is too much for you, just use the rule of thumb, that 5 miles in the hills takes about as long as 8 miles on the flat.

The route shown on the accompanying 1:100,000 maps is then described in detail with features that appear on the maps highlighted in **bold** in the text. Detailed maps show the route where it is sometimes difficult to find the way back to the route after taking a break to explore. Distances shown in brackets in the route description are the cumulative distance from the start of the stage and the distance still to ride to the end of the stage.

GPX tracks

GPX tracks for the routes in this guidebook are available to download free at www.cicerone.co.uk/987/GPX. A GPS device is an excellent aid to navigation, but you should also carry a map and compass and know how to use them. GPX files are provided in good faith, but neither the author nor the publisher accept responsibility for their accuracy.

LÔN LAS CYMRU

NCN fingerpost near Tregoyd where the Cardiff and alternative Chepstow start converge (Stage 1)

STAGE 1
Cardiff to Glasbury

Start	Sustrans marker post in front of the Wales Millennium Centre (ST 192 746)
Finish	Glasbury Bridge (SO 180 393)
Distance	70 miles (112km)
Ascent	1200m
Time	10–11hrs
OS maps	OS Landranger 160, 161, 170 and 171
Refreshments	Until Merthyr Tydfil you are never far from a shop or café although you will probably need to leave the route to find one. After that there is 20 miles with nothing near the route until you get near to Brecon and then another 9 miles with nothing until you get to Talgarth.
Accommodation	Plenty of accommodation of all types in Cardiff, Brecon and Glasbury.

This stage goes through the capital and up the Taff Valley following the largely traffic-free Taff Trail before climbing through the gap between the Brecon Beacons and the Black Mountains. There is a long easy descent into Brecon followed by a few miles of undulating hills before dropping down to meet the River Wye at Glasbury.

The impressive steel and copper front of the Wales Millennium Centre

The impressive **Wales Millennium Centre** (Canolfan Mileniwm Cymru), designed to express 'Welshness', incorporates materials that have played an important role in the history of Wales, such as slate, copper and steel. It is clad in slate from various quarries including those at Corris near the route of Lôn Las Cymru. The centre's main feature, the bronze coloured dome, is steel treated with an oxide of copper – both metals that were once economically important to South Wales. If you venture inside the building you can see how the principal internal spaces make extensive use of native hardwoods from renewable woodland in Mid Wales through which we will be riding.

Inscribed across the front of the dome are two poetic lines by the Welsh poet Gwyneth Lewis, one in Welsh and one in English. The one in Welsh reads 'Creu gwir fel gwydr o ffwrnais awen' (Creating truth like glass from inspiration's furnace) and was inspired in part by the furnaces from Wales's industrial heritage. The one in English reads 'In these stones horizons sing' and reflects both the traditional importance of the sea for exporting Welsh goods and the role of the building being a space for celebrating the very best of Welsh and other cultures.

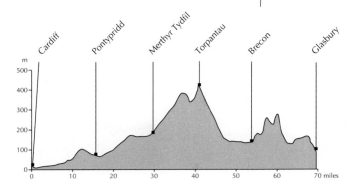

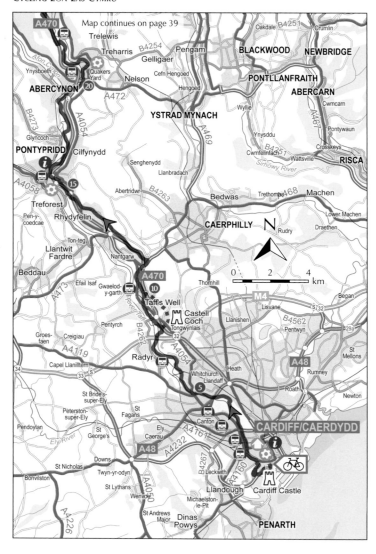

Map continues on page 39

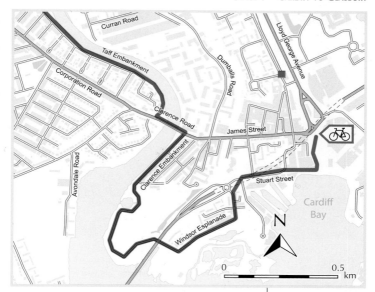

▶ From the Sustrans marker post, head across Mermaid Quay to the seafront and follow the shared-use path along Stuart Street, Dudley Street, Windsor Terrace, Windsor Esplanade and through the tunnel under the A4232 into Hamadryad Park. Ride through the park and

Although the Taff Trail follows the same route as National Cycle Route 8 until Brecon, both appear to have their own start points albeit only a few metres apart.

The sustrans marker post in Roald Dahl Plass, Cardiff Bay

THE SCOTTISH CONNECTION

Medieval re-enactment in front of the original Norman keep inside Cardiff Castle

Having left Cardiff where being Welsh is celebrated in the arts, sport and everyday life, it's perhaps safe to suggest that none of this would have happened without one particular Scottish family that the Welsh themselves still hold dear to their hearts. For centuries, the Earls of Bute had lived quietly on the island in the Firth of Clyde from which they took their title. All that changed in 1766 when the 4th Earl, and 1st Marquess, married the Honourable Charlotte Jane Windsor, who bought Cardiff Castle and large ancestral estates in South Wales into the family.

In 1801, Cardiff had population of 1870 making it only the twenty-fifth largest town in Wales, well behind Merthyr Tydfil and Swansea. John Crichton-Stuart (1793–1848), the 2nd Marquess of Bute, soon changed its fortunes when he exploited his mineral reserves and developed the docks and transport connections. Cardiff soon became the main port for exports of coal and iron from the Valleys and the city's population grew at a rate of nearly 80 per cent per decade between 1840 and 1870. The 2nd Marquess's investments paid off handsomely and he would later be known as 'the creator of modern Cardiff'. By the 1881 census, Cardiff had become the largest town in Wales. It became a city in 1905 and the capital in 1955.

His son, the 3rd Marquess of Bute (1847–1900), gained an inheritance that reportedly made him the richest man in the world. During his relatively short life he used his wealth to pursue his passions, which included medievalism and architecture, renovating and expanding both Cardiff Castle and Castell Coch, which are two of the finest examples of the late Victorian era Gothic Revival. The Marquess's patronage was also extensive and there is a park and many streets named after the family showing just how highly esteemed the name Bute is in the city.

along Clarence Embankment. Keep to the shared-use path and turn left along Clarence Road, crossing the River Taff for the first time. Once over the bridge, cross at the pedestrian crossing and follow Taff Embankment, Taff's Mead Embankment, Fitzhamon Embankment and Coldstream Embankment for 2 miles using pelican crossings to cross main roads.

The busy city centre with its famous landmarks such as Cardiff Arms Park and Cardiff Castle lies across the river. For the moment this bank is decidedly residential. Continue cycling past sports clubs and through Pontcanna Fields before crossing Blackweir Bridge to follow the route on the opposite bank through the northern end of Bute Park. The route sticks close to the River Taff for the next 4 miles. Then after passing first under the M40 motorway and shortly afterwards the A470 Cardiff to Glan Conwy Trunk Road, it moves away from the river through **Tongwynlais** (9/61 miles). At the end of Iron Bridge Road, turn left on to the A4054 Merthyr Road and follow it through the centre to join a shared-use path once beyond its boundary. ▶

To visit Castell Coch turn right up Mill Road in the centre of Tongwynlais and follow signs to the castle. Continue on this loop to re-join the main route just before Nantgarw.

The roads ahead are busy so stick to the shared-use path and designated crossings to navigate first the roundabout and then Cardiff Road before turning right into Taffs Well. Continue northwards using the shared-use path. Then, just before a mini-roundabout, cross at a blue fingerpost and follow the path alongside the opposite carriageway and over the **A470**. After 1½ miles of traffic-free cycling on what was clearly once a railway, cross the A468 dual carriageway in **Nantgarw** using the pelican crossing. Then follow signs around the corner into

Heol-y-Dderwen and then turn immediately right into Heol-y-Gors to re-join the track of the old railway.

Enjoy the next 5 miles of easy cycling with nothing other than a couple of minor roads to cross and a few access barriers to squeeze through. Once back on the road near the University of South Wales Glyntaff Campus, join the shared-use path, cross the roundabout and ride down Cemetery Road before crossing to the shared-use path alongside Pentrebach Road. Eventually the path becomes too narrow for cycling and you will need to resort to the road. After ½ mile turn left into Ynysangharad Road. At its end, a brown sign shows there is a busy roundabout to negotiate so turn left to pick up a shared-use path and use the designated crossings to get first to the north end of Ynysangharad Park and then across to shops on the north side of the A4223. ◀ Turn left into West Street at the end of the shops, then quickly right in South Street and subsequently into Middle Street and Bonvilston Road. At its end turn left along Coedpenmaen Road where once again the route follows the course of the old railway.

To visit the centre of Pontypridd follow Bridge Street downhill and cross the River Taff.

The fortunes of **Pontypridd** (16/54 miles) were inextricably tied to the coal and iron industries. Its position at the junction of three valleys made it an important location for the transportation of coal from the Rhondda Valley and iron from Merthyr Tydfil and its railway platform is thought to have once been the longest in the world during its heyday with trains passing through every two or three minutes. Since the decline of heavy industry, Pontypridd, in common with many other nearby towns, faces the overwhelming challenge of finding new industries to replace those that, for a century and half, provided employment for many thousands of people.

It is traffic-free cycling for the next 3 miles to **Abercynon** (19/51 miles) where the route emerges at a blue fingerpost. Ride along Martins Terrace and turn left on to the A4275 in front of The Navigation Inn and then

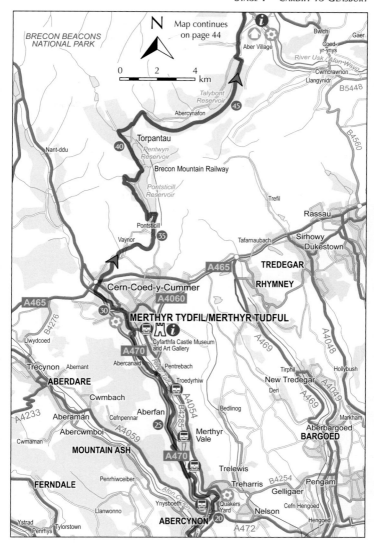

This lane – Tramway Road Side – commemorates Richard Trevithick who ran the first steam locomotive along tracks here on 21 February 1804.

quickly right by the fire station once again following the route along the course of the old railway. Within ½ mile, the route passes first under the A470 then shortly afterwards the A472. Continue up this narrow lane that circles around an islet in the River Taff called **Quakers Yard** where a community of dissenters buried their dead in the 17th century. ◄

The 200 metres beyond the railway viaduct can be muddy if it has rained. At its end, turn left past Pontygwaith Farm, which sometimes operates as a café, and cross the Grade II listed bridge over the River Taff that featured as a location in an episode of the BBC's 'Merlin'. Climb steeply uphill, dismount and walk through the gloomy tunnel under the **A470** turning sharply right soon after you emerge. A mile further on, pass under the A470 again and turn sharply left following the route along the hillside behind **Aberfan** (25/45 miles).

The majority of colliery spoil heaps along the Taff Valley have been flattened and landscaped. However, their disappearance will never erase memories of the **Aberfan disaster** that occurred on 21 October 1966 when a spoil heap collapsed and engulfed the school and neighbouring houses killing 116 children and 28 adults. The white arches in Bryntaf Cemetery on the hillside above the trail mark the graves of children who lost their lives in the disaster.

Continue northwards, crossing minor roads that occasionally snake up the hillside and pass under the A4060 and through the village of **Abercanaid**. Follow the path around the perimeter of a retail park on the outskirts of **Merthyr Tydfil**, passing under the A4102 and through the town's college campus. Cross the River Taff and turn immediately left towards Cefn-Coed-y-Cymmer along a shared-use path. Follow this path alongside the river then cross to Bethesda Street using the designated crossing on the corner. Turn left along Bethesda Street and go over the River Taff and then Cyfarthfa Road at the designated crossing. Two hundred metres further on, turn right into an unnamed road and follow signs down towards the river.

Follow the shared-use path, across the waste ground where Cyfarthfa Ironworks once stood, then a mile later over the Cefn Coed Viaduct across the river.

CYFARTHFA IRONWORKS

The remains of Cyfarthfa Ironworks alongside the route just south of Merthyr Tydfil

The massive archway across the waste ground bridges the gap in a bank of six iron furnaces built in the 1880s. They are all that remains of Cyfarthfa Ironworks (1765–1926), which, at its peak in the early 19th century, was a leading supplier of iron, cannon and cannon balls to the British Navy, employing thousands of workers.

Like much industry in South Wales, they were started by an outsider, Anthony Bacon (1716–1786), a Cumbrian by birth who eventually partnered with Richard Crawshay (1739–1810), a London iron merchant who had previously acted as Bacon's agent for supplying iron cannon to the Board of Ordnance. In the early 19th century, the output of Cyfarthfa was so critical to the success of the war effort that Horatio Nelson paid a personal visit to the works in 1802 and the immensely wealthy Crawshay family incorporated a pile of cannonballs in its crest. Subsequent Crawshays built Cyfarthfa Castle high above the town on the opposite bank of the River Taff which today houses the town's museum and art gallery. If you wish to visit it continue to follow Lôn Las Cymru northwards for a mile to Cefn-Coed-y-Cummer and then follow the brown tourist signs to the castle.

41

Turn right along High Street in **Cefn-Coed-y-Cyummer** and quickly left in Old Drill Hall Road. At its end, follow the shared-use path to the left of St John the Baptist Church and then ride for three traffic and junction-free miles alongside Taf Fechan (the little Taff) to emerge on a minor road in **Pontsticill** (35/35 miles). Turn left, cycle downhill passing under the railway bridge before turning left across the 110ft-high embankment of the **Pontsticill Reservoir** that since its completion in 1927 has been holding back 3400 million gallons of water.

The narrow-gauge **Brecon Mountain Railway** runs up the reservoir's eastern side along part of the route of the former standard gauge Brecon and Merthyr Railway. The railway, which was officially opened in 1863, was always financially stretched but struggled on until 1962 when it was axed during the Beeching cuts.

At present, the railway terminates at Torpantau at the northern end of the Pentwyn Reservoir which lies beyond the Pontsticill Reservoir to the north. The terminus is just short of the southern entrance to the 610m-long Torpantau Tunnel, which at an elevation of 400m above sea level was the highest standard gauge tunnel in regular use anywhere in Great Britain. The trustees of the Brecon Mountain Railway have an ambition to extend their line through the tunnel. However its poor condition would make restoration costly.

You can enjoy a 3-mile ride on the railway with your bike from Pontsticill station to Torpantau rejoining Lôn Las Cymru when you disembark. For timetables and fares, see www.bmr.wales.

Follow the road left at the end of the embankment. After 275 metres turn right towards Talybont-on-Usk, and then after another 275 metres, turn left and follow the trail through the Taf Fechan Forest. ◄ At the end of the trail, turn left along the undulating road along the western shore of the **Pentwyn Reservoir** which was constructed

The tarmac surface soon becomes gravel but is mostly well drained.

between 1858 and 1862 to supply clean water for Merthyr Tydfil which had suffered from repeated cholera epidemics. ▸

After 1½ miles, turn right immediately after crossing the Taff Fechan river and ride uphill past the picnic site. Turn left along the road at the end of this short trail, cross the cattle grid and continue climbing up and over the col at **Torpantau**. Descend for 450 metres, then turn right following marker signs into a conifer plantation. Enjoy this trail which runs downhill above the Talybont Reservoir for the next 5 miles giving fine views of the Brecon Beacons across the valley.

Cross the embankment at the northern end of **Talybont Reservoir**, turn right towards Brecon and enjoy another 2 miles of downhill cycling. Shortly after **Aber Village** turn left towards Llanfrynach and continue downhill to meet the B4558 at Cross Oak (48/22 miles). Turn left towards Llanfrynach and then a mile later just as you enter **Pencelli**, turn left towards Plas Pencelli. Turn left at the junction by the church in **Llanfrynach** then continue until once again meeting B4558. Turn left

During the 1849 cholera outbreak there were over 1000 deaths in one month alone.

Looking west towards the Brecon Beacons from the track above Talybont Reservoir

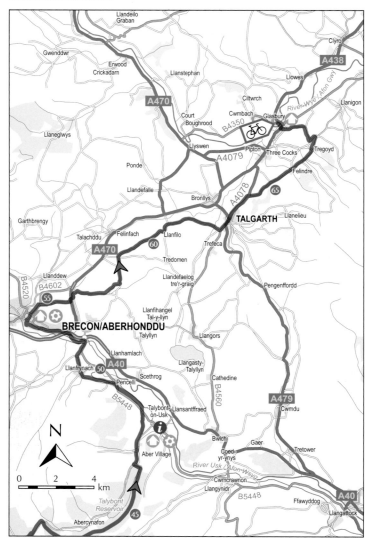

towards Brecon, then ⅓ mile later after first crossing the River Usk, turn left to follow the towpath alongside the Monmouthshire and Brecon Canal all the way to **Brecon** (55/15 miles).

Near the end of the canal, leave the towpath and follow route signs along Canal Road and around Theatr Brycheiniog. Then turn right at the mini-roundabout in Rich Way and left at its end along Watton. Filter into the middle lane as you reach the Brecon Museum and Art Gallery and turn right into Free Street. Cross the ring road at the traffic lights and ride up Cerrigcochion Road for ½ mile before turning right at the roundabout after the town's leisure centre and then immediately left into a narrow lane.

Brecon is a thriving little town that probably became established due to it being one of the few

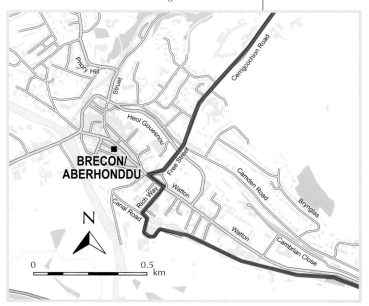

places where the river could be forded. Its Welsh name – Aberhonddu – is derived from the River Honddu, which meets the River Usk near the town centre. The Normans built a castle on the hill and defensive walls around the town, but they were largely destroyed during the English Civil War. Once Brecknockshire was absorbed into Powys in 1974, Brecon lost its status as county town but remains a thriving community with an important cattle market and plenty to entertain the large influx of tourists who flock into the area. Their numbers are boosted in early August when the town hosts the internationally acclaimed Brecon Jazz Festival. See www.breconjazz.org for details.

Brecon lies at the north of the Brecon Beacons National Park. The park was established in 1957 and covers 519 square miles. It stretches from Llandeilo in the west to Hay-on-Wye in the north-east and Pontypool in the southeast.

Turn left a mile later after passing through the tunnel under the A470, then right 200 metres later. Turn right again at the next junction and then a mile later turn left; all of these turns are indicated by route markers. Turn left at the end of this lane in front of an isolated house whose owners enjoy fine views of the Black Mountains. There is no route marker at this junction for those riding north-wards but look back once past Drostre Nature Reserve to see one for those riding south.

After ½ mile turn right into a narrow lane near a green agricultural building. Again the route marker at this junction is temporarily absent perhaps because it was attached to a telephone pole that has been recently replaced. Go straight across the next junction, where route signs reappear and climb up the steep, southwestern slope of Penyrallt before descending to **Llanfilo** (61/9 miles).

Follow the road around the well-preserved church that is dedicated to a local saint named Bilo and ride down through the village before turning right towards

Talgarth. Turn left on to the B4560 and then after 200 metres join the shared-use path. You can either stick to this path alongside the busy A470, before turning right towards Three Cocks or follow signs through the Talgarth town centre which has a working watermill and a 14th-century defensive tower house.

The well-preserved Norman and medieval church in Llanfilo viewed through the lychgate

> In the fifth century **Talgarth** was the residence of Brychan, an Irish born prince who married Marchel, a Welsh heiress to become the King of Brycheiniog from which Brecon gets its name. According to legend, Brychan was married three times and fathered 22 sons and 24 daughters including Bilo to whom the church at Llanfilo is dedicated.

Follow the shared-use path that runs alongside the **A4078** for a mile outside the village then turn right towards Felindre. Ride through **Felindre** and the hamlet of **Tregoyd** a mile further on until you come to a prominent blue fingerpost at a crossroads where NCR8 and NCR42 intersect. Turn left, following markers for NCR8 towards Glasbury. After the bend, turn right again. Then after ¾ mile bear left. A mile later, turn right at the cross-roads in Tyruched. Once you meet the **A438**, cross to the shared-use path on the opposite carriageway and turn right to **Glasbury**.

NORTH TO SOUTH

If riding north to south stock up on food in Brecon ready for the 25 miles to Merthyr Tydfil and use the NCR8 extension from Cardiff Bay to the station if you are taking the train.

STAGE 1A
Chepstow to Glasbury

Start	Chepstow Old Bridge (ST 536 944)
Finish	Glasbury Bridge (SO 180 393)
Distance	57 miles (91km)
Ascent	1500m
Time	9–10hrs
OS maps	OS Landranger 161, 162 and 171
Refreshments	Chepstow, Shirenewton, Usk, Abergavenny, Llananthony, Hay-on-Wye and Glasbury.
Accommodation	Hostels only in Chepstow, near Abergavenny and in Glasbury but a good selection of B&Bs and hotels in the major centres.

Once you leave Chepstow you are immediately on quiet lanes through what remains of the ancient Wentwood before dropping down to follow the River Usk northwards to the pleasant market town of Abergavenny. Beyond that comes the delightful Vale of Ewyas, which culminates in a short climb through the Gospel Pass – the highest in Wales – that gives breath-taking views northwards into central Wales and the English Marches. After an enjoyable descent through the literary town of Hay-on-Wye, it is easy riding to Glasbury.

Chepstow gets its name from the Old English *chepe stowe*, meaning a market place or trading place, and during the Middle Ages it was a major centre for importing wine from Europe and exporting timber from nearby woodlands. As the larger ports of Cardiff, Swansea and Bristol became more prominent in the early 19th century, Chepstow's importance diminished. However, its picturesque location at the mouth of the River Wye meant trade was replaced with tourism which remains an important part of the town's economy today. Old Wye

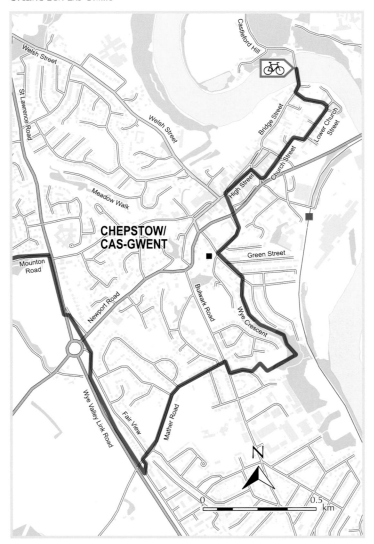

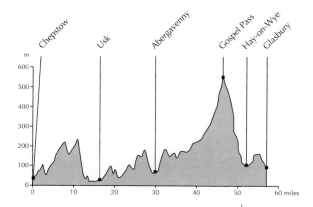

Chepstow | Usk | Abergavenny | Gospel Pass | Hay-on-Wye | Glasbury

Bridge, from where the stage begins, is an elegant iron structure cast by John Rastrick of Bridgnorth in 1816. Chepstow Castle, which is the southern-most of a chain of border castles, was built by the Normans soon after their victory at the Battle of Hastings in 1066.

Old Wye Bridge in Chepstow

51

Once off the Old Wye Bridge, bear left and follow the one-way system along Church Street into the town centre and left up High Street. Turn left onto a narrow path immediately before the 13th-century Town Gate and follow it across Mount Pleasant and along Garden City Way with remains of the old town walls to your left. Follow route markers left along Hardwick Avenue then right into Wye Crescent which narrows to become a shared-use path that emerges on Strongbow Road. Turn right at the junction with Bulwark Road, then immediately left along Mathern Road passing first the Chepstow Athletic Club and then the town's cemetery.

Turn left up Maple Avenue, just before the tunnel under the Wye Valley Link Road. Then turn right onto a shared-use path that runs adjacent to its southbound

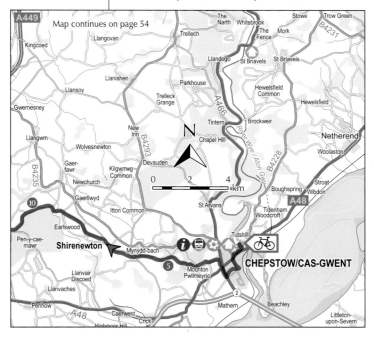

carriageway. Follow this path around the busy Highbeech Roundabout, first on the town side of the main road, then crossing to the other carriageway. Turn left into Mounton Road and ride away from the town and towards the open country. At a mini-roundabout about a mile further on, the NCR4 turns left towards Newport, while we turn right towards Shirenewton following signs for NCR42.

It is steady climbing up to Shirenewton (6/51 miles) with progressively improving views of the Severn Estuary and Bristol Channel to the south. ▶ Turn right towards Usk at the paved area in the centre of the Shirenewton. Two miles outside the village, turn left towards **Earlswood** and ride through this tiny hamlet. Turn left at the first crossroads and then right at the next crossroads following signs towards Llantrisant and Usk.

Stop at the next junction by Pen-y-cae-mawr Chapel (11/46 miles) and enjoy the wonderful view of the Black Mountains and the rolling Herefordshire countryside to the north. It is a just reward for the climb up from the coast. And there is another treat around the corner when you cycle down the 15% hill into the Usk Valley passing under the busy A449 and through **Llanllowell** into **Usk** (16/41 miles). Follow the route along Church Street and Priory Street into Twyn Square. Then turn left at the junction with the A472 and quickly right into Portycarne Street following signs for Abergavenny.

Enjoy these views while you can because you will soon be riding along sunken lanes under a dense canopy of foliage where vistas are briefly caught through field gates.

In recent years **Usk** has achieved considerable success in Britain in Bloom competitions, with Her Majesty's Prison Usk, which today finds itself in a very suburban setting on the right as you enter the town, contributing to the display. With a number of pubs, restaurants and antique shops, and a fine bridge and the remains of a 12th-century castle, it really ought to be more popular as a tourist destination. But perhaps visitors are deterred by the volume of traffic that passes through the centre on its way to and from the more industrial towns to the west.

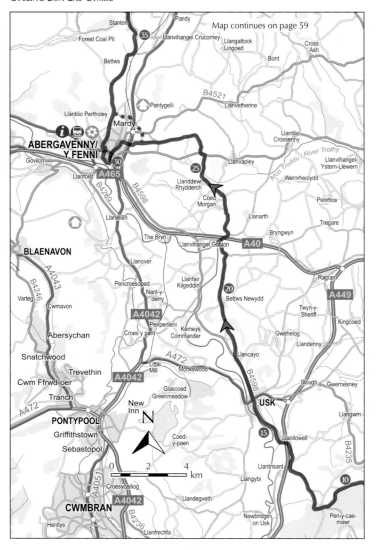

Map continues on page 59

Pen-y-cae-mawr Chapel, with the Black Mountains in the background

Once you reach **Llancayo** (18/39 miles) turn right towards Bettws Newydd. ▶ Pass through **Bettws Newydd**, although a pretty village there is little reason to stop unless the pub is open, and after 2 miles turn left in front of the late 18th-century Gothic gatehouse of Clytha Park, a 19th-century neoclassical country house hidden in the woods. After less than a mile, turn right towards Llanarth and then once across the bridge over the M40, turn left towards Llandewi. It is a quiet lane running between low hedges that gives good views west to the hills on the opposite bank of the River Usk and east towards the rolling Herefordshire countryside. After a mile, turn right towards **Coed Morgan**, a tiny hamlet that is just off-route to the left. Turn left at the next junction following a route marker sign and cycle gently downhill into **Llanddewi Rhydderch** (25/34). Once through the village turn right into an unnamed road and follow it for a mile to the junction with the B4233. A small marker post next to the mail box on the left confirms you should turn left. Then less

Look back to see the 19th-century Llancayo Windmill which since restoration is available for self-catering holidays.

55

than 100 metres further on, another sign partially hidden in the hedge confirms you should turn right.

Follow this narrow lane for 2 miles emerging at a crossroads by a fruit farm. Bear left around a triangle of grass and take the lane immediately opposite. If you look back you will see a route marker to confirm you are on route. Half a mile further on there is a prominent finger-post that indicates a shortcut around Abergavenny that saves just 2 miles.

Shortcut via Llantilio Pertholey

Turn right at the fingerpost (SO 319 149) following direc-tions for Llanthony. Cross the B4521 and then ignore the route markers for NCR46 and continue through the tun-nels under the A465 and railway and through **Llantilio Pertholey**. Next cross the Hereford Road and follow this lane for ½ mile to a T-junction. Turn right to re-join the main route heading towards Pantygelli and Bettws.

Continue downhill towards Abergavenny, riding through the tunnels under the A465 and railway before turning left onto Ross Road. At the end of this little-used lane, turn left into Lower Monk Street. Then turn right into a park just before a bridge over the small Gavenny River. At the end of the park, cross the busy Monmouth Road and follow the shared-use path around into Mill Street. Turn left into a cul-de-sac alongside Mill Street Industrial Estate and follow the shared-use path around to Castle Street. Then turn right into the partly pedestrianised Nevill Street before dismounting and walking through the town centre. Shortly after encountering traffic again in Frogmore Street, turn right into a narrow lane oppo-site the bank that soon broadens out to become Queen Street. Use the pelican crossing to cross Penyfal Road, turn right into Park Avenue and then left into Skirrid Road. At its end, turn right and immediately right again into Park Crescent. Then turn left into a narrow lane just after a block of garages and right once you meet the Old Hereford Road.

Abergavenny became an important centre both for the Romans and the Normans due to its location at the confluence of the Gavenny River and the River Usk. The town was granted the right to hold two weekly markets and three annual fairs in the 13th century and that tradition continues today with local produce, crafts and antiques for sale in the busy Market Hall on most days. The annual Abergavenny Food Festival reinforces the town's reputation as a mecca for foodies and you will find plenty of tempting gastro pubs, cafés and restaurants. In recent years the town has hosted the Abergavenny Festival of Cycling with an evening criterium for the professionals, a sportif and a number of events for leisure cyclists. For details see www.abergavennyfestivalofcycling.co.uk.

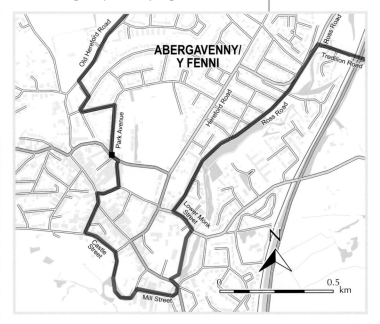

Alternative route through the town centre

The serpentine route is waymarked throughout. However it is remarkably easy to become disorientated. So you can just head into the town centre to browse the shops and enjoy coffee and cake. Then head up through the town centre towards the war memorial, cross and take Pen-Y-Pound Road that runs to the right side of the prominent Baptist Chapel. This eventually becomes the Old Hereford Road.

There is a short climb around the southwestern flanks of Sugar Loaf, but once past **Pantygelli** (33/26 miles) pedalling becomes easier. Turn left in Penyclawdd following signs for Cwmyoy and St Llanthony and left again a mile later to reach **Stanton**. Just beyond the village the road swings to the northwest running alongside Afon Honddu along the Vale of Ewyas. It is a steeply banked road through a continual tunnel of hazel, oak and ash so views are few and far between. However, you soon catch a glimpse of the village of Cwmyoy across the valley and it is worth making a detour to visit.

The Church of St Martin on the wooded hillside at Cwmyoy

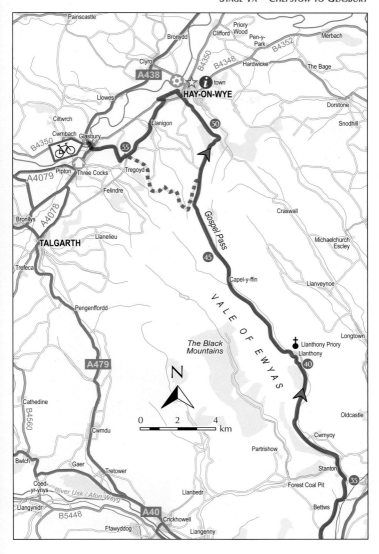

The ruins of the early 12th-century Augustinian priory at Llanthony

The largely 13th-century Church of St Martin at **Cwmyoy**, tucked in the wooded slopes of Hatrall Hill on the opposite bank of Afon Honddu, is reputed to be the most crooked church in Great Britain. The local geology consists of Old Red Sandstone lying over marl, and over the centuries, slippage and subsidence have caused the tower and chancel to move in opposite directions, twisting the entire structure. You can ride a loop through the village by turning right as soon as you see its name on a signpost and re-join the route a mile further on.

There is more ecclesiastical interest 3 miles further on at **Llanthony** (40/19 miles) where there are the ruins of an early 12th-century Augustinian priory.

The deposed Edward II stayed at Llanthony Priory on 4 April 1327 on his way to Berkeley Castle, where he is assumed to have been brutally murdered. The priory was once one of the most important medieval buildings in Wales but its fortunes were already in decline before the Dissolution of the Monasteries. Its infirmary was converted into St David's Church and other buildings were turned into a private house and subsequently a hotel. Court Farm Barn, the original gatehouse of the Priory, is a few hundred metres to the north.

Three miles further on at **Capel-y-ffin** (44/15 miles), where the valley starts to narrow, is the tiny 18th-century St Mary's Chapel, which also has a twisted tower. ▶ Gradually the trees become stunted, the hedges are less dense and you start to get views across open moorland of windswept bracken and heather. Ahead lays **Gospel Pass** (47/12 miles) which at 549m (1801ft) above sea level is the highest road pass in Wales. The miles of barely perceptible climbing since Abergavenny leaves only a couple of hundred metres of ascent and it rarely gets above 5% gradient – unlike that from the north which is both longer and steeper.

Its graveyard contains a headstone engraved by the sculptor and designer Eric Gill (1882–1940) who during the 1920s lived at nearby Capel-y-ffin Monastery, now a private residence.

Gospel Pass (Bwlch yr Efengyl), which squeezes between the summits of Lord Hereford's Knob

Wild ponies on the slopes below the Gospel Pass

(690m) to the west and Hay Bluff (677m) to the east, is said to get its name from 12th-century crusaders who travelled this way – a plausible explanation as Llanthony Priory is just a few miles away down the Vale of Ewyas. What no one knows is how Lord Hereford's Knob got its name. However, what really matters is the view you get from the col. It runs all the way from the Brecon Beacons in the west around to the Cambrian Mountains in the north and seems to go on endlessly across the rolling Herefordshire countryside to Shropshire and beyond.

Although the road surface is good, watch out for walkers, sheep and ponies on the glorious 5-mile descent to Hay-on-Wye (52/7 miles).

Shortcut to avoid Hay-on-Wye

If you are a bibliophobe or behind schedule you can avoid Hay-on-Wye saving 3½ miles by turning left at a route marker 1½ miles after leaving the top of the Gospel Pass. It is a narrow lane with a ford and a short, steep descent just before the junction with NCR8.

There is an excellent cycle shop and café on a small industrial estate as you enter the town.

◀ On reaching **Hay-on-Wye**, turn right into Church Street towards the town centre, then quickly left into Swan Bank alongside the hotel and follow this residential lane past the parish church to meet the busy B4350.

Hay-on-Wye (Y Gelli Gandryll) owes its popularity to bookseller and self-proclaimed 'King of Hay', Richard Booth, who in the 1970s pioneered the selling of second-hand and specialist books as a way of boosting the town's economy. It was an inspired move and today the town has numerous bookshops, specialist retailers and eateries and its annual literary festival is internationally renowned.

Turn left back towards the town, then after 275 metres turn right towards Llanigon. Ride through **Llanigon** (54/5 miles) until you come to a prominent blue fingerpost 1½ miles beyond the village where NCR8 and NCR42 intersect.

Turn right, following markers for NCR8 towards Glasbury. After the bend, turn right again. Then after ¾ mile bear left. A mile later, turn right at the crossroads in Tyruched. Once you meet the A438, cross to the shared-use path on the opposite carriage and turn right to the bridge in **Glasbury** where the stage ends.

NORTH TO SOUTH

If riding north to south be prepared for two climbs. First comes 5 miles (8km) up the Gospel Pass from Hay-on-Wye at an average 5% gradient with short sections getting into double figures. Then after Usk is a 1½-mile (2.5km) climb at Pen Y Cae Mawr at an average gradient of 8% with a short section above 15%.

Whiling away time in one of the many bookshops in Hay-on-Wye

STAGE 2
Glasbury to Llanidloes

Start	Glasbury Bridge (SO 180 393)
Finish	Old Market Hall, Llanidloes (SN 956 845)
Distance	48 miles (77km)
Ascent	1000m
Time	7–8hrs
OS maps	OS Landranger 148, 147 and 136
Refreshments	Boughrood, Erwood Station, Builth Wells, Newbridge-on-Wye, Rhayader and Llangurig.
Accommodation	Plenty of hostels, although those near Rhayader are a few miles off route, and plenty of other types of accommodation in the towns.

This is a stage of two halves: the first is easy going alongside the River Wye to Builth Wells, then you encounter some gradients as you get into the Cambrian Mountains. The climbs are never long or particularly steep but they are persistent. If you feel you would be happier with a more relaxed schedule, you should allow more time for Stage 2, and possibly Stage 3, which is equally demanding. It will also give you more time to enjoy the glorious countryside, watch wildlife such as common buzzards and red kite which are now quite numerous in central Wales, and explore the little market towns.

The River Wye once split **Glasbury** – a village once famous for its apple orchards – between the counties of Radnorshire and Brecknockshire. It was not a happy relationship and following a dispute over the cost of constructing a new bridge in 1850 the village was left with one that was half-wooden on the Radnorshire side and half-stone on the Brecknockshire side. When county boundaries were reorganised in 1974 the entire village became part of Powys.

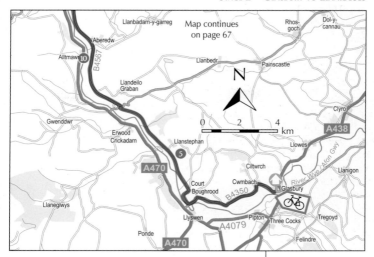

Map continues on page 67

Once across the bridge, turn left towards Boughrood and ride through the hamlet of Boughrood Brest following the course of the River Wye, which is out of sight on your left. Once you reach **Boughrood** (3½/44½ miles) turn right into Station Road towards Painscastle and ride through the village and then through **Llanstephan** where the wooded sides of the valley start to get steeper. It is

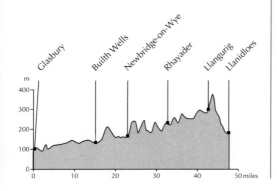

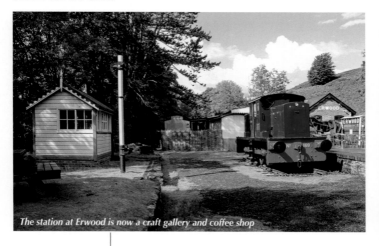

The station at Erwood is now a craft gallery and coffee shop

Formally opened in 1864, the 47-mile line was never busy and by 1888 had been absorbed into Cambrian Railways eventually being closed in the 1960s.

easy cycling however as the road incorporates much of the track bed of the old Mid Wales Railway that ran from Brecon through Builth Wells to Caersws. ◄ Turn left towards Aberedw once you meet the B4567. Then, if you like railways, crafts or coffee, pull in at Erwood Station (8/40 miles) where old Great Western coaches form much of the gallery space and there is a Fowler 0-6-0 industrial diesel locomotive and other railway memorabilia.

There are few houses around here because this quiet road was built over a railway line. Three miles further on, the small village of **Aberedw** lies a few hundred metres off route. Continuing ahead is **Llanfaredd** (13/35 miles) where there is only a farmhouse and a little church.

The last sovereign **Prince of Wales**, Llewelyn ap Gruffydd (1223–1282), lived at the 11th-century Aberedw Castle. It is hidden in the trees before the turn for the village although there is little to see as its ruins were destroyed when the railway was built.

Turn left towards Builth Wells when you meet the A481. Then after about 350 metres, turn left at the

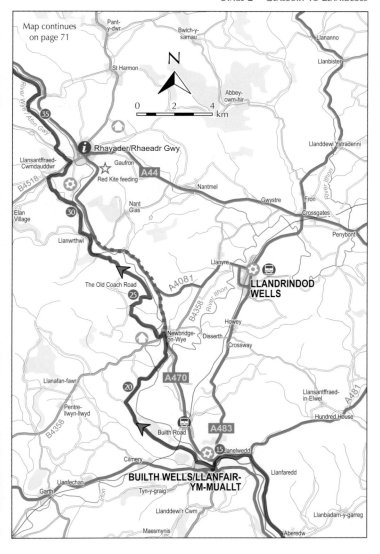

Map continues
on page 71

N

0   2   4
km

River Wye / Afon Gwy

Pant-y-dwr

Bwlch-y-samau

Llananno

Llanbister

St Harmon

Abbey-cwm-hir

35

i Rhayader/Rhaeadr Gwy

Llansantffraed-Cwmdauddwr

B4518

Gaufron

Red Kite feeding

A44

Llanddewi Ystradenni

Nantmel

Gwystre

Fron

River Ithon

Nant Glas

Crossgates

Penybont

30

Elan Village

Llanwrthwl

Llanyre

Llandrindod Wells

A4081

The Old Coach Road

B4358

River Ithon

25

Howey

Disserth

Newbridge-on-Wye

Crossway

Llanafan-fawr

A470

20

Pentre-llwyn-llwyd

B4358

Builth Road

A483

Llansantffraed-in-Elwel

A481

Hundred House

Cilmery

15 Llanelwedd

BUILTH WELLS/LLANFAIR-YM-MUALLT

Llanfaredd

Llanfechan

Tyn-y-graig

Garth

Ithon

Llanddewi'r Cwm

Maesmynis

Aberedw

Llanbadarn-y-garreg

67

roundabout and ride through the industrial estate to follow a shared-use path into **Builth Wells** (15/33 miles). At the end of this path, turn left along Station Road and ride over the bridge into the town. Follow the road around into Broad Street and up High Street before turning right into Strand Street. At its end, turn right along The Strand, past the town's war memorial and immediately left after the pedestrian crossing into The Groe, the town's riverside park.

Builth Wells is one of the few points where the River Wye can be forded making it an important stopover from drovers who once walked herds of cattle from West Wales to markets in England. The arrival of the railway in the middle of the 19th century enabled the town to exploit local mineral waters and promote itself as a spa, eventually tacking the word 'Wells' to its name. During the second half of the 19th century visitors flocked to Builth to 'take the waters' and a myriad of hotels, guest houses and shops were built to accommodate them. Today the

Some of the 11,000 sheep at the September auctions in Builth Wells

town is home to Wales's Royal Agricultural Show, one of the largest in Europe, which takes place over four days in July attracting more than 200,000 visitors into the area. At other times of year the showground hosts other fairs and sporting events as well as regular livestock auctions. See www.rwas.wales for details.

Ride through the pleasant avenue of trees alongside the River Wye to meet a small bridge over the River Irfon. Cross the bridge then turn right along Golf Links Road steadily climbing with the River Wye once again to your right. After 3 miles, turn right towards Newbridge-on-Wye and follow this quiet road for 3 miles. Turn left along a stretch of shared-use path, then join the A470 for ½ mile and cycle down through the centre of **Newbridge-on-Wye** (23/25 miles) before turning left into Llanafan Road. Turn left at its end, cross the River Wye and turn right towards Llysdinam. Climb uphill for just over a mile and follow the road around as it swings northwards at an isolated junction. Then after 350 metres, turn right at a T-junction and ride back down into the valley.

After a mile the road becomes a track called the Old Coach Road that skirts along the bracken covered hillside for the next 2 miles. Its surface is mostly rough gravel although after heavy rain it can become muddy, particularly the final 200 metres. You will have to dismount to navigate a few gates and you may decide it is better to walk some parts of it which seems a better option than riding for 5 miles along the busy A470 trunk road between Newbridge-on-Wye and Llanwrthwl that Sustrans suggest as an alternative.

Across the River Wye at the foot of Rhiw Gwraidd is **Dowdowlod House**, which was built by James Watt junior (1769–1848), the only surviving son of the famous inventor James Watt (1736–1819) who bought a farm here in 1785. They still own it today making it available for weddings and private events.

Once through the final gate of the Old Coach Road, ride downhill into the small village of **Llanwrthwl** (28/20 miles). Turn left by St Gwrthwl's Church, where there is a standing stone about 1.75m (5ft 9in) high near the south porch, and then turn right towards Elan Village on the outskirts of the village. Follow this quiet lane for 3 miles around the wooded slopes of Carn Gafallt with the River Wye to the right below the scarred slopes of Gwastedyn Hill (477m/1565ft). ◀

The residents of Rhayader race up Gwastedyn Hill during their annual carnival week.

Turn right at its end, cross the iron bridge over the Afon Elan and then turn right through a gate at the junction with the B4518 and follow this shared-use path through the woods and wildlife reserve. Pass through the elaborately carved gate. ◀

To visit Rhayader (just off route) turn right and ride through Cwmdauddwr, across the bridge over the River Wye and into town.

Rhayader was once a stopping place for monks travelling between the abbeys of Strata Florida to the west and Abbeycwmhir to the northeast. Drovers also passed through driving their livestock to markets in the Midlands. Perhaps that is why the town has the highest concentration of pubs per head of population of any town in the UK, with one to every 173 people.

Leaving Rhayader with the rocky nose of Gamallt prominent above the opposite bank of the River Wye

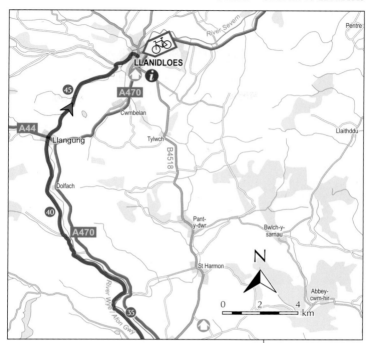

Today Rhayader is an important centre for tourists visiting the impressive reservoirs and dams in the nearby Elan Valley and those wanting to see red kite. There is a Red Kite Feeding Centre on the southern edge of the town where you can watch them at close quarters. However these elegant birds are no longer rare and you may see them anywhere between Builth Wells and Machynlleth soaring on their curved wings and twisting their long forked tail to change direction.

Turn left and then right following signs for Aberystwyth Mountain Road. After 550 metres of climbing, turn right into a narrow lane which swings around

LLANIDLOES

The half-timbered Old Market Hall in Llanidloes

The first town on the River Severn, Llanidloes was once an important centre for flannel. Before the 19th century it was a cottage industry and many of the three-storey houses in the town would have housed weaving lofts on the upper storey. Mechanisation shifted production into mills, such as the one by the River Seven. The new technology was far from profitable and production dwindled resulting in a local Chartist revolt in 1839. Its ringleaders were arrested, tried and sentenced to imprisonment or transportation. The last mill closed in 1913.

The half-timbered Old Market Hall was built around 1600 and is the only surviving building of this type in Wales. Assize courts were held in the upper hall during the 17th century and John Wesley preached from a pulpit stone on the open ground floor in 1748. Today Llanidloes looks like a traditional market town but still retains a reputation for radicalism and quirkiness making it a popular retreat for those seeking an alternative lifestyle, much like neighbouring Machynlleth.

to the northwest following the course of the River Wye. It is pleasant riding past fields of grazing cattle with the conical summit of Gamallt (475m/1560ft) prominent on the opposite bank. Pass through an isolated farmyard and some farm gates. Turn right at the end of this lane, then immediately left towards Dernol and continue for 5 miles crossing the River Wye for one final time before **Llangurig** (43/5 miles) which has a café, shop and two pubs. ▸

Turn left at the post office and then immediately right at the pub. After a mile of gentle climbing, keep right at the junction and descend into the next valley. Ride through the scatter village of Glynbrochan and across the bridge over the River Seven to a prominent fingerpost. ▸ Turn right into **Llanidloes** which is ½ mile off route; you will see the Old Market Hall, which is the end point of this stage, once you cross the bridge over the River Wye.

Enthusiasts of railway trivia know Llangurig as having the shortest-lived line in the UK, receiving precisely one goods train before the Manchester and Milford Railway Company abandoned it due to financial difficulties in 1864.

If you are not stopping, turn left to continue.

NORTH TO SOUTH

If you are riding north to south apart from a short climb out of Llanidloes you will be mostly cycling downhill following the course of the River Wye.

STAGE 3
Llanidloes to Dolgellau

Start	Old Market Hall, Llanidloes (SN 956 845)
Finish	Bont Fawr, Dolgellau (SH 729 179)
Distance	39 miles (62km)
Ascent	1200m
Time	7–8hrs
OS maps	OS Landranger 136, 135 and 124
Refreshments	Staylittle (just off route), Machynlleth and Corris.
Accommodation	Good selection of accommodation in all the towns along the route.

This is undoubtedly the wildest stage of the route with the first climb over Foel Fadian going above 500m (1640ft) and the second across the bwlch below Myndd Y Waun above 400m (1312ft). Opportunities for acquiring refreshments are sparse so carry provisions with you. Needless to say, riding through the high mountains makes for a memorable day.

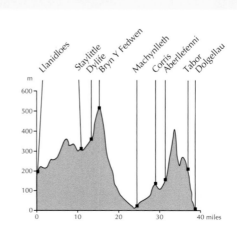

Head west along Short Bridge Street, cross the River Seven then bear left into Penygreen Road and follow this narrow road for the next 10 miles. It is gentle climbing initially with the River Seven on your left. Then once within the boundaries of the Hafren Forest the road swings northwards away from the river close to its source on the lower slopes on nearby Plynlimon (752m/2467ft) which is the highest summit in Mid Wales.

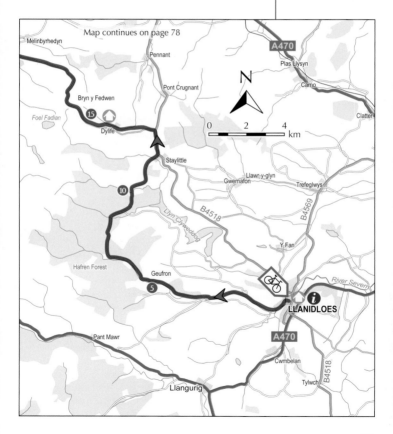

Map continues on page 78

75

The impressive Ffrwd Fawr waterfall

The **Hafren Forest**, which covers around 15 square miles, consisted of pine and spruce when it was planted in 1937 but in recent decades native species have been introduced to create greater biodiversity and more varied habitats for wildlife. The seeds of the conifers attract flocks of crossbills that feed high up in the tree tops and the newly planted areas make ideal habitat for nightjar. But the outstanding success in recent years has been a pair of ospreys successfully rearing young at a site on Llyn Clyweddog, adjacent to Lôn Las Cymru.

Shortly after leaving the forest, turn left near **Staylittle** (11/28 miles), an isolated village with such patchy mobile coverage it is reputed to attract visitors looking for a 'digital detox'. Ride along the B4518 for a mile, then turn left towards Machynlleth. After ½ mile, there is a viewpoint into the V-shaped Dylife Gorge which was formed as a U-shaped valley during the last ice age but was further eroded by the fast-flowing River Twymyn. ▶

The 40m-high Ffrwd Fawr waterfall is tucked out of sight at the bottom of the Dylife Gorge below the viewpoint.

Ride on through **Dylife** (14/25 miles), where lead was mined until the end of the 19th century, and climb gently for 3 miles up the southwest slopes of **Foel Fadian** (564m/1850ft) reaching an altitude of 512m on the col between the summit and **Bryn Y Fedwen**.

Along the road to the northeast of the summit of **Foel Fadian** is a memorial to the broadcaster Wynford Vaughan-Thomas (1908–1987) who was president and chairman of the Campaign for the Protection of Rural Wales between 1968 and 1975. Built from local slate, the memorial is in the form of a toposcope looking out over the rolling hills and mountains to the north with Snowdon, Wales's highest peak, just visible on a clear day.

After an enjoyable view, comes 8 miles of downhill to Machynlleth. There are no junctions but take care as you will meet farm traffic and possibly a golfer as the road passes through the town's course. At the end of the road, turn left into the centre of **Machynlleth** (24/15 miles).

The monument to Wynford Vaughan-Thomas high above the Dovey Valley near Machynlleth

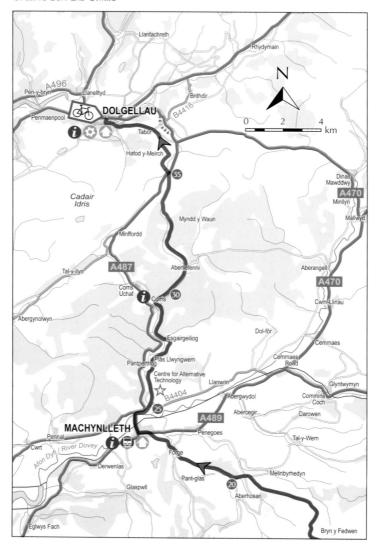

Although small, **Machynlleth** has big ambitions. Because the Welsh prince Owain Glyndŵr held a parliament here in 1404, the town claims to be the 'ancient capital of Wales', but in 2000 and 2002, it unsuccessfully applied for city status. It is unlikely that many of the town's residents mind, because since the 1960s Machynlleth has been a magnet for those seeking an alternative lifestyle. Lôn Las Cymru passes the Centre for Alternative Technology, which was set up in an old slate quarry in 1973 to pioneer ideas about sustainable living that are now mainstream. Hidden in the trees above

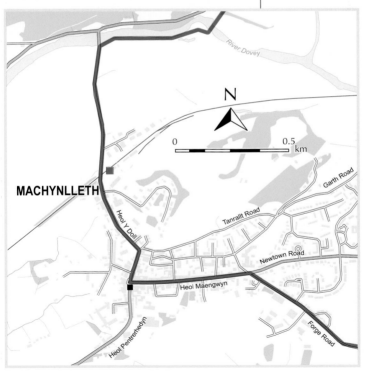

The Millennium Bridge, built to create a safe route for pedestrians and cyclists

the bridge over the River Dovey is Bron-Yr-Aur, a privately-owned 18th-century cottage where the rock band Led Zeppelin wrote and recorded part of their third album. Not everyone who came stayed. But some did, setting up a wide selection of shops, cafés and small businesses that give the town its distinctive and still slightly alternative feel.

Ride down the broad Heol Maengwyn, turn right towards Dolgellau at the clock tower and ride past the railway station joining a shared-use path that leads to the River Dovey. Turn right just before the old bridge and follow the path to the Millennium Bridge, which was built on the site of an old railway bridge so cyclists and walkers can avoid a hazardous section of the A487. Once you meet the road, continue along the shared-use path then turn right on the B4404 towards Llanwrin. Once over the bridge across the Aber Glesyrch, turn left towards the Centre for Alternative Technology. What follows is 9 miles of ascent but the route runs adjacent to the course of the old Corris Railway so gradients are fairly gentle.

It is pleasant riding beneath a canopy of mixed woodland with views of the conifer plantation across the narrow valley. Ride through the small village of **Esgairgeiliog**, (27/12 miles) and on to **Corris** (29/10

THE CORRIS RAILWAY

The Corris Railway was built in the 1850s to carry slate from quarries at Corris and Aberllefenni down to wharves on the River Dovey. Initially horses hauled carriages along a tramway, but they were replaced by locomotives once the line was upgraded to standard gauge in the 1870s. This allowed passengers to be carried and in the late 1880s the railway promoted itself to tourists as being the best route to the summit of Cadair Idris using horse-drawn carriages to offer a circular 'Grand Tour' that linked Corris station to Abergynolwyn station on the nearby Talyllyn Railway.

After World War I, the slate industry declined due to cheaper imports and the increasing popularity of alternative roofing materials. The line became unprofitable and by the time UK railways were nationalised in 1948, erosion along the banks of the River Dovey meant parts of the southern section of track were unsafe and the railway was closed. Since 1966 dedicated enthusiasts have restored what was left of the railway, opened a museum and are gradually reviving the line.

miles). It is the last place on this stage with either a shop or a café. ▶

Continue northwards passing through **Aberllefenni** (32/7 miles) where almost everything possible is constructed from slate including houses, fences and patios.

Until 2016, most of the properties in **Aberllefenni** were owned by the descendants of John Lloyd, who established the Inigo Jones Slate Works at Y Groeslon near Caernarfon in 1861 primarily to supply writing slates for schools. At its peak in 1890, Aberllefenni Slate Quarry employed 190 men but was already in decline when the Lloyd family acquired it in the 1950s to supplement dwindling supplies at their northern quarries. Records show that slate had been extracted at Aberllefenni since before 1500 so by the time quarrying stopped in 2003 it was the longest continually operated slate mine in the world. Today only the slate mill remains in use, processing slate from quarries in Blaenau Ffestiniog and Penrhyn.

The latter is only open during the summer months, so you may have to leave the route, ride through the village to the café at the Corris Craft Centre which is open all year.

The restored office building at Hengae Slate Quarries in Aberllefenni; the bell here was rung to signal the end of a shift

The Mach Loop – the valleys between Machynlleth and Dolgellau – is used by the Royal Air Force and the US Air Force for low-level training, see **www. machloop.co.uk**.

If you are not stopping in Dolgellau but continuing onto the next stage, follow the route markers around the car park to pick up the path alongside Afon Wnion.

Turn left on a corner just after the recently restored mine office and ride up Cwm Hen-gae past the ruins of old quarry buildings. The gradient steadily increases into the mid-teens first as the road enters the forestry and again once it has left it. It is also difficult to settle into a rhythm as there are gates to pass through every so often. But on a clear day your efforts are rewarded with fine views of Cadair Idris (893m) to the west and Snowdonia to the north. ◀

The surface across the bwlch below **Myndd Y Waun** is generally excellent, but do take care to control your speed on the descent as there are gates. Cross the A487 using the designated crossing and the short stretch of cycleway, then turn left and pass through a gate to follow the route up past the farm at Gwerngraig and the houses at Hafod-y-meirch. After a short climb, the road descends through woodland to join a minor road above the hillside village of Tabor. Turn left and ride through **Tabor** (37/2 miles) and steeply downhill into **Dolgellau**. Turn left and ride along Arran Road into the town following marker signs along Finsbury Square, Stryd Fawr and Bridge Street to **Bont Fawr** (the big bridge), where the stage ends. ◀

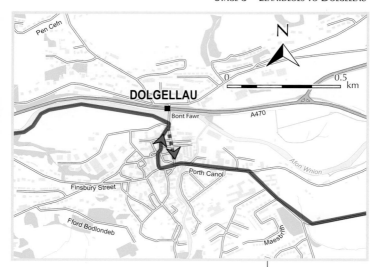

Weaving wool was an important activity in **Dolgellau** until the 19th century, when mechanical looms put an end to hand looms. So too was tanning, but that died out in the 1980s shortly after Dolgellau lost its administrative status as the county town of Merionethshire and became part of Gwynedd. However, its position at the foot of Cadair Idris, the second most-popular mountain in Wales after Snowdon, means Dolgellau has a thriving economy based on tourism, although agriculture still plays a role with a popular farmers' market taking place on the third Sunday of every month.

NORTH TO SOUTH

If you are riding north to south be prepared for two big climbs, first for 1½ miles (2km) out of Dolgellau at an average gradient of 8%, then for 8 miles (12km) out of Machynlleth which is fairly gentle until the corners at the top where gradients exceed 10%.

STAGE 4
Dolgellau to Caernarfon

Start	Bont Fawr, Dolgellau (SH 729 179)
Finish	Caernarfon Castle (SH 477 577)
Distance	60 miles (96km)
Ascent	1100m
Time	9–10hrs
OS maps	OS Landranger 115 and 124
Refreshments	There are plenty of places for food stops except on the high level section between Llanfair and Penrhyndeudraeth and the 10-mile stretch between Llanystumdwy and Penygroes.
Accommodation	Hostels in Dolgellau, Barmouth, Garndolbenmaen (on the shortcut) and Caernarfon, and plenty of B&Bs and hotels all along the route.

The Mawddach Trail gives an easy start but after Barmouth you need to make some choices about which route to take. There are three main options: to avoid Harlech on the standard route, to avoid Harlech on a high-level unsigned route or to visit Harlech. The easiest option is to forego Harlech and follow the high-level route, which has less severe ascents that the other two options. After that it is easier riding through the towns and villages along Tremadoc Bay before crossing the Llŷn Pensinsula, where there is an optional shortcut saving 8 miles, before following the Lôn Eifion path to Caernarfon.

If for any reason you want an alternative, exit to the nearby A493 and re-join Lôn Las at Morfa Mawddach Station.

Start at the 17th-century **Bont Fawr** (the big bridge), and ride around the car park to pick up the route which runs between the playing field and Afon Wnion. At the end of the rugby pitches, cross the footbridge and follow the path along the north bank of the river, across the A493 and over a second footbridge to join the Mawddach Trail. ◄

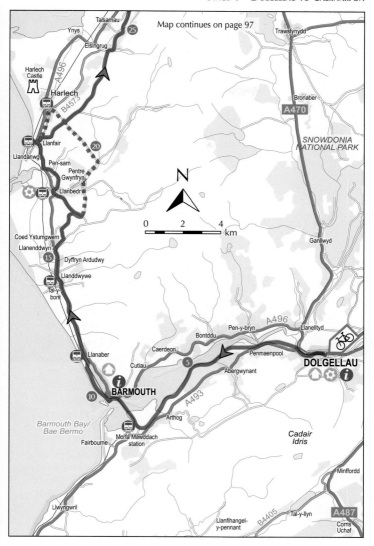

Map continues on page 97

The toll bridge across the Mawddach Estuary at Penmaenpool

The **Mawddach Trail** follows the route of the Cambrian Line (1867–1965) that ran across Wales from Ruabon to Barmouth via Bala. It is a shared-use path which winds for 9½ miles along the disused railway track on the southern edge of the delightful Mawddach Estuary. It is flat with a good gravelled surface and for most of its length is at least 3 metres wide giving plenty of room for passing. To the north there are stunning views of Diffwys (750m) and the Rhinogs. You may also catch sight of the rocky summit of Cadair Idris (893m) to the south through gaps in the foliage. But there is plenty of interest nearby.

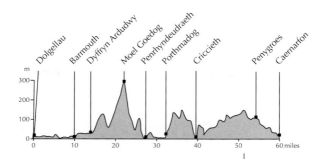

Much of the estuary is listed as a site of special scientific interest with two RSPB reserves (Taicynhaeaf across the toll bridge on the north shore and Arthog just before Morfa Mawddach Station) as well as a visitor centre housed in a railway signal box at Penmaenpool, where spotting scopes and binoculars are available to use.

Turn right at the end of the trail and ride past Morfa Mawddach Station and across Barmouth Viaduct. This

Looking south from Barmouth along the viaduct across the Mawddach Estuary

87

largely wooden viaduct, which was opened in 1867, carries the Cambrian Coast Railway across the estuary. It is a remarkable structure but after half a mile of riding across the uneven timbers you will look forward to getting off it just as much as you did to getting on it.

At its end, go through a gap in the wall, turn left and ride down Porkington Terrace into **Barmouth** (9/51 miles). Turn left onto The Quay and ride under the railway and around to The Promenade. You can enjoy traffic-free cycling on the shared-use path right along the seafront. At its end, take another shared-use path, across the railway and up to join the A496. Turn left and follow this road for 4 miles enjoying views of the Llŷn Peninsula across Cardigan Bay.

BARMOUTH

In the 16th century Barmouth was a small port for coastal vessels trading grain, timber, wool and locally-caught herring. Trade increased during the following centuries, particularly the shipping of timber used for the manufacture of pit props, and to support it Barmouth became an important centre for ship building. During the 18th century, local merchants built elegant Georgian homes, some of which can be seen on the town's Heritage Trail.

The town was already attracting well-to-do travellers with an appreciation of picturesque landscapes including the poet William Wordsworth (1770–1850), who after a visit in 1824 wrote 'With a fine sea view in front, the mountains behind, the glorious Estuary running eight miles inland, and Cadair Idris within compass of a day's walk, Barmouth can always hold its own against any rival.' No one could possibly disagree with him including holiday-makers from the industrial towns of the Midlands and North West who started to visit once the railway arrived in 1867. In the 20th century, the traditional factory summer holiday closures saw a dramatic increase in the number of tourists with special trains bringing thousands of factory workers and their families to the coast. Although the train still brings tourists to Barmouth, today the majority come by road; the fast 'A' roads from the Midlands and the North West making the resort easily accessible for day trippers.

Turn right in **Dyffryn Ardudwy** (15/45 miles) towards Cwm Nantcol and climb Ffordd-y-Brws for ½ mile. Then turn left following a route marker at the corner of a stone wall. Follow this narrow lane for a mile until you come to a junction where a marker sign indicates that NCR8 turns left.

High-level alternative

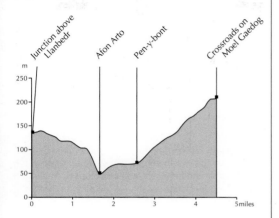

It is here that you can take advantage of an unsigned, but easier and picturesque high-level option. Turn right and after 200 metres turn left and follow the road gently downhill into the woodland at **Coed Aberartro**. Cross the bridge over Afon Cwmnantcol and immediately afterwards another longer bridge across Afon Artro. Turn right after the second bridge and follow the road uphill towards Cwm Bychan with the river to your right. After passing through **Pen-y-Bont**, where a public telephone box and a post box are the only notable features, turn left towards Harlech. After climbing gently for 1½ miles, turn right towards Talsarnu to re-join the main route.

Follow the NCR8 signs, and turn left and ride down the narrow and occasionally twisty lane into **Llanbedr** (18/42 miles), which is a pleasant village with both a coffee shop and a bike shop. Turn right along the **A496** and then just

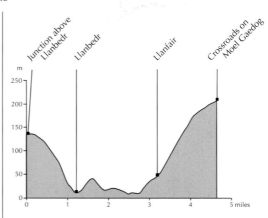

after crossing Afon Artro, turn right towards Cwm Bychan. Turn left by the war memorial and cycle up through the trees to meet another quiet lane that drops to re-join the A496. Turn right onto the shared-use path and follow it into **Llanfair** (20/40 miles).

Turn right at marker signs on the outskirts of the village and climb gently up the southwest ridge of Moel Goedog which gives good views of the Rhinogs to the southeast. Once over the crest you also get a glimpse of Harlech Castle and glorious views across the estuary to the mountains of Snowdonia. You can now enjoy 3 miles of descent, but take care as there are patches of gravel and a couple of gates to negotiate.

For an easier climb, retrace your steps back along Ffordd Uchaf to re-join the route at the junction just north of Llanfair and turn left to climb the southwest ridge of Moel Goedog.

The route via Harlech

From **Llanfair** follow Ffordd Uchaf for a mile to the outskirts of Harlech, turning right along Stryd Fawr enjoying panoramic views down across the bay. One waymarked route out of Harlech goes straight up Pen Dref, the steep hill on the opposite side of the castle, giving a mile of climbing at a gradient of 10% and more especially on the lower slopes. Once at the junction, turn left to re-join the standard route. ◄

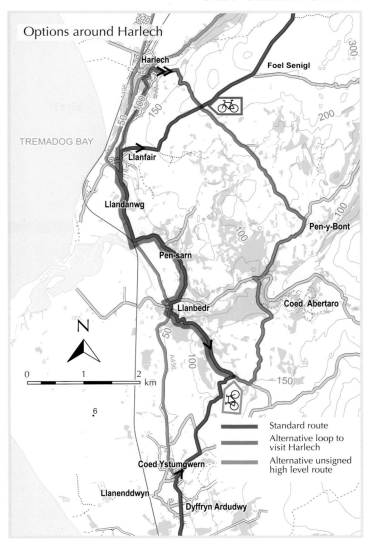

Options around Harlech

Harlech
Foel Senigl
300
150
100
50
200
TREMADOG BAY
Llanfair
Llandanwg
100
Pen-y-Bont
Pen-sarn
100
Llanbedr
Coed Abertaro
N
50
A496
0   1   2 km
100
150
·6

Coed Ystumgwern

Llanenddwyn
Dyffryn Ardudwy

Standard route
Alternative loop to visit Harlech
Alternative unsigned high level route

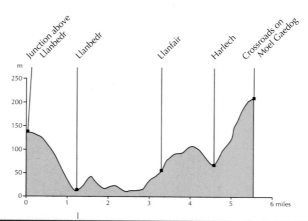

HARLECH CASTLE

Parked up below Harlech Castle

When Edward I started building Harlech Castle in 1283 during his invasion of Wales, it was on the coast, but centuries of silt deposits have left it stranded inland on a rock outcrop that was once a sea-cliff. Over the centuries, the castle has had many occupants. Owain Glyndŵr (1359–circa 1415), the last unofficial king of Wales, captured the castle in 1404 and held it until 1409 when it was retaken by English forces. Lancastrian forces held the castle for seven years during the Wars of the Roses (1455–1487), from 1461 until Yorkist troops forced them to surrender in 1468 during what is thought to have been the longest siege in the history of the British Isles famously commemorated centuries later in the song 'Men of Harlech'. Forces loyal to Charles I held the castle from the outbreak of the English Civil War in 1642 until 1647 when it became the last fortification to surrender to the Parliamentary armies, who subsequently destroyed the gatehouse staircases to make the castle unusable.

Since then the castle has been a picturesque ruin attracting visits from prominent landscape artists including JMW Turner. The United Nations Educational, Scientific and Cultural Organization (UNESCO) gave the castle World Heritage status in 1986 declaring it one of 'the finest examples of late 13th century and early 14th century military architecture in Europe'.

The northern slopes of Moel Goedog provide 4 miles of almost continual descending but you will need to look out for farm gates and the junction in the tiny hamlet of **Eisingrug** where the route forks right. Cross the A496 at **Cilfor** and ride along the shared-use path over the River Dwyryd to **Penrhyndeudraeth** (28/32 miles). ▶

Turn right opposite the railway station, cross the A487 at the designated crossing in the village centre and ride along Stryd Fawr for just less than 150 metres before turning left into Pensarn opposite the village's car park.

From 1872 until 1997 explosives and munitions were manufactured in Penrhyndeudraeth; the site of the factory is now a nature reserve notable for nightjars in summer.

Cycling up Moel Goedog from the north with Porthmadog and Portmeirion across the estuary

Portmeirion from across the Dwyryd Estuary

Turn left at the end of Pensarn and then after 25 metres turn right and follow this narrow lane under the railway and the by-pass and then back over the railway.

Detour to Portmeirion

To visit Portmeirion, a round trip of 2½ miles off-route, turn left at the post box which shares an island with an NCR8 fingerpost by the cottages 275 metres after passing over the railway. Cross the A487 to the entrance to the village.

Portmeirion was built between 1925 and 1975 by local architect Clough Williams-Ellis (1883–1978). Inspired by Italian fishing villages, he also incorporated a collection of architectural relics in order to create a picturesque village in direct contrast to the utilitarian architecture of the time. Portmeirion rocketed to fame in the late 1960s when it featured as 'The Village' in the spy drama *The Prisoner*. It was only then that Williams-Ellis introduced an entrance fee as a way to prevent the village being spoilt by overcrowding. He died in 1978 and in accordance with his wishes, his ashes were scattered over the estuary by a marine rocket. Today a charitable trust runs Portmeirion which includes a hotel, self-catering cottages, shops, a café, tea-room and restaurant.

Turn right at its end and follow the shared-use path across Britannia Terrace past the terminus of the Festiniog and Welsh Highland railways and into **Porthmadog** (31/29 miles).

▶ Just after the harbour turn right into Madoc Street and then immediately right along Lynn Bach past the town's main car park re-joining Madoc Street once past the one-way system. At the end of this road, which

If you feel like a break, explore the town and then head for the town's railway station on High Street to re-join the route.

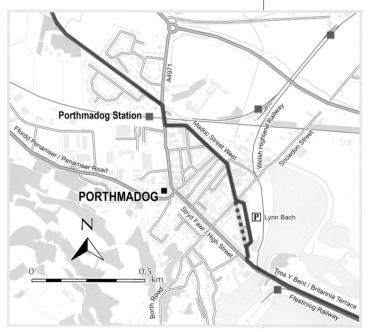

Porthmadog Station
Ffordd Penamser / Penamser Road
A4971
Madoc Street West
Welsh Highland Railway
Snowdon Street
PORTHMADOG
Stryd Fawr / High Street
P Lynn Bach
N
0   0.5
          km
Borth Road
Tros Y Bent / Britannia Terrace
Ffestiniog Railway

becomes Cambrian Terrace, turn right into High Street, and then turn left into Pensyflog immediately after the level crossing.

PORTHMADOG

William Madocks (1773–1828), a wealthy lawyer, acquired the Tan-yr-Allt estate on the western side of the Glaslyn Estuary in 1798 and immediately commissioned a 2-mile-long embankment across the upper estuary to create productive farmland. Fuelled by his success, Madocks set about building a second, 1450-metre-long stone embankment called 'The Cob' across the lower estuary. Soon after completion in 1812, the embankment was breached in a storm and subsequent repairs left Madocks with considerable debts. Undaunted he developed plans for a harbour at Porthmadog and a railway to Blaenau Ffestiniog, both of which came to fruition after his death when the abolition of duties on slate revitalised the industry. Today the town that Madocks created relies on tourism for its living. The wharves survive, but the slate warehouses have been replaced by holiday apartments and the harbour is used by leisure yachts. Meanwhile the town still celebrates William Madocks and both of his embankments remain in use, the first carrying the Welsh Highland Railway across the estuary and The Cob carrying the A487, the Ffestiniog Railway and more recently Lôn Las Cymru.

If you want a break, bicycles can be carried on the Welsh Highland Railway, which is the UK's longest heritage railway running for 25 miles from Porthmadog through the stunning Aberglaslyn Pass and the picture-postcard village of Beddgelert and past the foot of Snowdon to Caernarfon. However, space is limited so phone 01766 516024 to make a reservation before travelling.

Continue along Pensyflog alongside a ditch that drains land reclaimed from the estuary before passing through the tunnel under the A487. At the end of this now shared-use path, turn left along Dublin Street, then quickly right into a narrow road that also quickly turns into a shared-use path and follow it past the hospital and along the hillside to **Penmorfa** (33/27 miles). Turn right along Hen Ffordd and climb steadily uphill with views out over Cardigan Bay to your left. Turn right at the end of Hen Ffordd and continue climbing looking back to

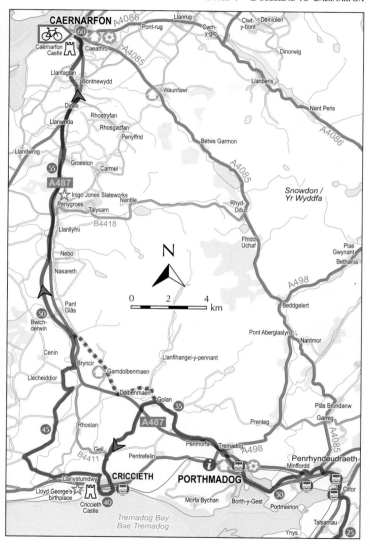

In the woodlands ½ mile north of Golan is the six-storey Gothic Brynkir Tower built by local landowner Sir Joseph Huddart to impress the future George IV who, as Prince of Wales, visited the area in 1821.

After assessment in 2008, this became the most westerly 2000-ft peak in Wales by a mere 5½ inches.

see Moel Y Gest (263m/863ft) which despite its modest height is an impressive hill. The climbing ends near the cemetery, then it is briefly downhill past the woollen mill and through **Golan**. ◄

Shortcut via Garndolbenmaen

If you are staying in Garndolbenmaen or need to recover lost time, there is a way-marked shortcut from just north of Porthmadog to the start of Lôn Eifion that avoids Criccieth saving 8 miles.

Turn right towards Garndolbenmaen at a finger-post 275 metres after passing Brynkir Woollen Mills. After ¾ mile, turn left by a white cottage immediately after crossing Afon Dwyfor and follow the road past the parish church in **Dolbenmaen**. Join a shared-use path on the right just before the junction with the A487 and follow it for just less than 150 metres alongside the main road and around into the minor road that leads to Garndolbenmaen. Ride into **Garndolbenmaen** and turn right on the bend by Capel Horeb. After 1½ miles, turn left by a farm and ride for 1½ miles gently uphill along the southwestern slopes of Mynydd Craig Goch (610m/2000ft). ◄ Turn left after passing the white cottage at Cwmbran and cycle downhill to meet the A487. Use the cycle path to cross the main road and then ride for ½ mile across the cattle grid and towards the quarry to re-join Lôn Las Cymru near the start of Lôn Eifion, the shared-use path that leads all the way to Caernarfon.

Fork left from Golan to meet the A487. Cross the junction and then after 2 miles turn left to join the **B4411** by a caravan park and enjoy a long descent into **Criccieth** (39/21 miles). Cross the busy A497 and then the railway line and follow the road through the village before turning right along Castle Street. After a short climb up past the castle, the road swoops downhill past the Victorian villas along Marine Crescent before turning back inland to cross the railway and the A497 at a staggered junction.

It is thought that the first castle at **Criccieth** was built by Llywelyn the Great (Llywelyn ap Iorwerth) (circa 1172–1240), who ruled most of Wales for 45 years. Much of the current structure, however, was built by Edward I at the end of the 13th century as part of a ring of castles surrounding his newly-conquered Welsh lands. The rebel Owain Glyndŵr (circa 1359–1415) briefly controlled the castle in the early years of the 15th century, but once it fell in 1404, part of the walls were torn down and both the castle and the town were burned.

The castle was never to be reoccupied so the town lost its importance until the arrival of the railway in 1867 gave it a new future as a resort. Notable holidaymakers included the Bird family, famous for their custard, who owned a villa called 'Foinavon' opposite the lifeboat station that the current owner has fittingly painted yellow.

Ride up the lane, turn left at the top and ride down into **Llanystumdwy** (42/18 miles) passing the riverside grave of David Lloyd George (1863–1945).

Lloyd George, the British Prime Minister from 1916 to 1922, spent much of his boyhood in the village and started his career articled to a firm of solicitors in nearby Porthmadog. You can visit the Lloyd George Museum in the centre of Llanystumdwy between April and October.

Turn right and cross the River Dwyfor and then after just over 350 metres turn right towards Plas Talhenbont Hall starting a gentle climb across the Llŷn Peninsula. Turn left towards Llangybi 100 metres later at an elegant lodge to the now ruined Gwynfryn Plas, a flamboyant mansion built by local landowner and MP, Sir Hugh John Ellis-Nanney (1845–1920) who was defeated in the parliamentary by-election of 1890 by the young Lloyd George.

Half a mile later cross the bridge over Afon Dwyfach and follow the road past the gatehouse of the 17th-century Plas Talhenbont Hall, which is now an exclusive wedding venue. Turn right at the next junction joining a regional cycle route and follow this winding road for 3 miles to its end, looking out for some substantial gateposts that were probably standing stones before being repurposed in the days before heritage conservation.

Turn left and follow this road for a mile, past a seemingly deserted farmyard at **Llecheiddior**. Then turn right, ride through the evidently busy farmyard at Llecheiddior Uchaf and down the twisting concrete drive to the livestock market and industrial units on the site of the old station at **Bryncir** (48/12 miles).

From here for 12 miles to the end of the stage in Caernarfon, the route follows Lôn Eifion, following sections of track bed of the former Carnarvonshire Railway that were not incorporated into the A487 that runs parallel. Unless there is a headwind, progress is rapid especially if you are in a group and get into a rhythm negotiating the numerous gates. For the most part, you will be oblivious to the villages served by the line – Pant Glâs, Penygroes, Groselon, Llanwnda, Dinas and Bontnewydd – that are just to the east. A sign on the route just after **Penygroes** (53/7miles) directs you to the **Inigo Jones Slate works** and its café, which is adjacent to the route. ◄

The historic Grade I listed gardens of Glynllifon Park are 2 miles off-route to the west of Groeslon.

Use the designated crossings to negotiate the busy roundabout just south of **Llanwnda** (57/3 miles). Otherwise just enjoy the views of Snowdon at the end of the Nantlle Valley to the east and the remaining few miles of traffic-free cycling into right to the car park below Caernarfon Castle where the stage ends.

The building of **Caernarfon Castle** began in 1283 during the reign of Edward I and was completed in 1330 during the reign of his grandson Edward III. Despite appearing to be a well-preserved castle, none of the interior buildings survive and many planned buildings were never finished. When Henry VII (1457–1509) seized the English

The outwardly impressive Caernarfon Castle

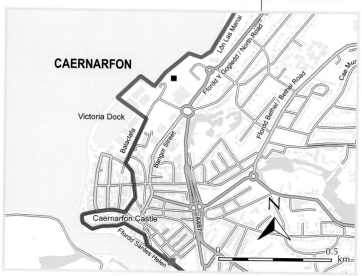

CAERNARFON

Victoria Dock

Caernarfon Castle

crown after the Battle of Bosworth in 1485, his Welsh ancestry help legitimise the Tudor's rule over Wales, and tensions diminished and the castle fell into disrepair. Despite its dilapidated condition, it was occupied by the Royalists during the English Civil War (1642–1651) and was besieged three times before the garrison finally surrendered to the Parliamentarian forces in 1646. It was the last time Caernarfon Castle saw conflict.

The government started to fund repairs to Caernarfon Castle in the late Victorian era when it became the accepted location for investing the title of Prince of Wales on the British monarch's heir.

NORTH TO SOUTH

If you are riding north to south you can easily visit Harlech. However, take care down Pen Dref, the steep hill that leads directly to the castle, as it is twisty, has gradients of 10% and more, and ends at a busy junction.

STAGE 5
Caernarfon to Holyhead

Start	Caernarfon Castle (SH 477 577)
Finish	Maritime Museum Holyhead (SH 245 833)
Distance	38 miles (61km)
Ascent	500m
Time	5–6hrs
OS maps	OS Landranger 114
Refreshments	Once past Menai Bridge, where there is an ample supply of pubs and an excellent supermarket, there is nothing directly on the route other than shops at Llangaffo (18 miles) and Bethel (22 miles) until you get close to Holyhead.
Accommodation	Plenty of accommodation in the towns but not much along the quiet lanes on Anglesey.

This is an easy stage through pleasant countryside with plenty of opportunity to visit the tourist attractions along the way. First comes the old quay at Y Felinheli where slate was once loaded to destinations around the world. Then comes crossing the Menai Straits by the historic suspension bridge before winding through the quiet lanes of Anglesey to a dramatic finish on top of the cliffs above South Stack Lighthouse.

Start from the car park by the footbridge across the Afon Seiont and cycle around the castle, through the archway and up Castle Ditch. As you approach Castle Square, turn left down Greengate Street alongside the town walls, underneath the Eastgate archway and down Bank Quay. Turn right into Glan Mhor opposite North Gate and ride along Balaclafa Road joining a shared-use path that leads around the perimeter of Victoria Dock car park and northwards along the coast.

The route then joins Lôn Las Menai, a 4-mile section of dismantled railway that linked Caernarfon with the old slate harbour of Y Felinheli (Port Dinorwig). It is pleasant cycling through broadleaf woodlands, briefly emerging to

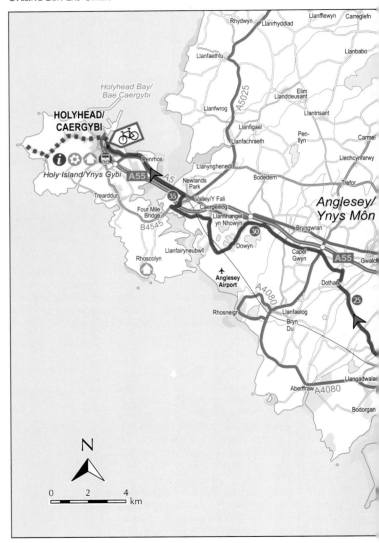

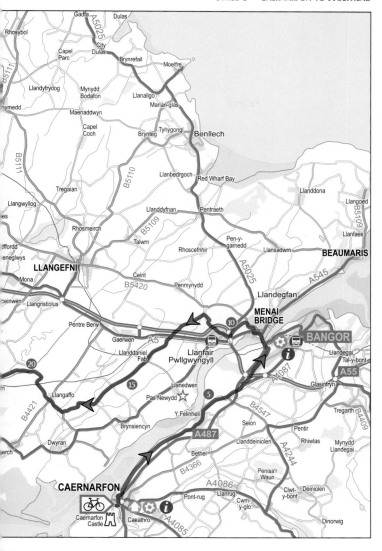

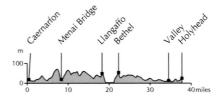

follow a shared-use path alongside and then parallel to the old Caernarfon Road before emerging on Beach Road in **Y Felinheli** (4/35 miles).

Turn left and ride down through the industrial units to the little seafront. Turn left at the corner by the Garddfon Inn and follow the route through the houses and along Hen Gei Lechi, past the old port which is now a busy marina. Turn left onto the cycle path just before the T-junction with the main Bangor road, then cross the main road again following the course of the old railway.

Within a mile the route re-joins the road. Then turn left at the T-junction with the B4547, take the shared-use path on the opposite carriageway and follow it right at the next junction following signs towards Bangor. Soon you have to cross to a shared-use path that runs along the opposite carriageway adjacent to the walls of Vaynol Hall.

Owner of the **Vaynol Estate**, Thomas Assheton Smith (1752–1828) became fabulously wealthy from slate quarrying. Early in the 19th century he developed the Dinorwic Quarry near Llanberis but it never flourished until he constructed a horse-drawn tramway to Port Dinorwic in 1824.

Later that century, when steam trains carried the slate, Dinorwic Quarry employed more than 3000 men and was the second largest opencast slate producer in the country. Production dwindled during the 20th century and stopped for good in 1969. Likewise the Assheton Smith family, which had amassed 36,000 acres of land by the start of the 20th century, gradually disposed of their estate and finally sold Vaynol Hall in 1984.

MENAI SUSPENSION BRIDGE

Menai Suspension Bridge from near Llanfair Pwllgwyngyll

Before the Menai Suspension Bridge opened in 1826, the only way to and from Anglesey was by taking the ferry across the fast flowing and dangerous waters of the Menai Strait. One of the most tragic accidents occurred in 1785 when 54 passengers drowned after a boat became stranded on a sandbar. Valuable cattle raised on the Anglesey also frequently perished as drovers swam them across on their way to mainland markets.

Eventually Thomas Telford (1757–1834) was commissioned to find a solution and he proposed a suspension bridge which would avoid having to build piers on the shifting sands of the sea-bed and be high enough to allow sailing ships to pass. The bridge has been strengthened many times, both to make it more stable in high winds and to cope with increased traffic. The growth in rail travel necessitated building the nearby Britannia Bridge which was designed and built by the engineer Robert Stephenson (1803–1859) and opened in 1850. Although it now carries the majority of today's traffic, it lacks the elegance of Telford's bridge which is a Grade I listed building and World Heritage Site.

Cross again after the roundabout following a path alongside the A487. At the top of the rise, turn right and ride over the A55 Expressway and into Penrhosgarnedd (7/32 miles) before turning left at a mini-roundabout. Turn right on the first bend following route markers into an unnamed lane. Then at its end, turn right towards Bangor following a shared-use path alongside the opposite carriageway. As you descend towards the Menai Straits the path narrows, so briefly join the road and then take the first exit at the roundabout towards Menai Bridge.

Stay on the left side of the road and cross the Menai Suspension Bridge (9/30 miles) on the shared-use path that faces the Britannia Bridge. Follow the path around the first roundabout then along Mona Road with the supermarket on the left and the Menai Heritage Centre on the right. Turn left towards Holyhead at the next roundabout, then cross to the shared-use path on the opposite side of the road and turn right up Cemetery Road past the cemetery and then, once the road turns into a path, Menai Bridge Cricket Club. Turn left on reaching Penraeth Road and follow the shared-use path past the leisure centre to the roundabout at Four Cross. Turn left along the A5025 following signs for Holyhead and continue along the shared-use path over the A55 North Wales Expressway to **Llanfair Pwllgwyngyll** (10/29 miles).

Llanfair Pwllgwyngyll, which is dominated by the Marquess of Anglesey's Column, is known by its original shorter name but is famous for its longer name: Llanfairpwllgwyngyllgogerychwyrndrobwll llantysiliogogogoch (Parish of St Mary in the hollow of the white hazel near the rapid whirlpool and the parish of St Tysilio with a red cave). This was conjured up to attract tourists once the railway arrived in the 1860s. Although it may not be used on the road signs its 58 characters still makes an imposing platform sign at the village station. No less eye catching is the wonderful panorama of Snowdonia across the Menai Straits enjoyed from the village on a clear day.

Once across the A55 North Wales Expressway, turn right into Lôn Refail and then right at the T-junction at the end into Ffordd Penmynydd and follow it once more across the A55 North Wales Expressway and into open countryside. Turn left towards Star at the T-junction and ride through this pretty village which enjoys expansive views of Snowdonia. Keep following this quiet road, once again over the A55 North Wales Expressway, across a staggered crossroads on the A5 and through to **Llanddaniel Fab** (14/25 miles). Two miles east of Llanddaniel Fab is Plas Newydd, a National Trust property that was once the country seat of the Marquess of Anglesey.

It is pleasant riding along quiet country lanes where you are only likely to meet a farm tractor, milk tanker or occasional local. Keep an eye out for the next NCR8 marker and turn right into a narrow lane at a post box on a staggered crossroads. ▶

At the end of this meandering lane, turn right along the B4419 and ride into **Llangaffo** (18/21 miles) where there is a village shop. Cross to the small road next to the

Near the top of the rise, look right to see Bodowyr Burial Chamber, just a short walk off the road, built as a passage grave in Neolithic times when the remaining stones would have been covered with earth.

Bodowyr Burial Chamber, Anglesey

109

shop and ride downhill, under the railway bridge and out to Malltraeth Marsh.

> **Malltraeth Marsh** is a large area of grazing and reed beds that was reclaimed in the early years of the 19th century. European water voles inhabit the marsh and birds such as lapwing, curlew, redshank and common snipe are common on the wet grasslands. Rarer visitors, such as the secretive Eurasian bittern, frequently over-winter here, but have yet to breed locally.

Turn left immediately after crossing Afon Cefni, then right after a mile and climb up through the small village of Trefdraeth and on to **Bethel** (22/17 miles). Turn left towards the village centre, where there is a shop, then quickly right towards Soar. As you ride downhill away from Bethel, you get the first glimpse of Holyhead Mountain at the end of the route.

Turn right at the next T-junction and follow the road for 3 miles through Soar, which appears to have no village sign, across the next crossroads following signs for Pencarnisiog and Bryn Ddu. Half a mile after **Dothan** (26/13 miles), turn left into a narrow lane and follow it for the next 4 miles, first crossing the A4080 in Engedi (28/11 miles) then a second unmarked crossroads near the A55 Expressway.

Turn left at the T-junction and ride up Minffordd Road through **Llanfihangel Yn Nhowyn** (31/8 miles) and around the perimeter of RAF Valley which is a magnet for plane spotters. Once over the railway, take care not to miss a concealed turn into Lôn Ty Main; just before an electricity substation. Follow this lane over the railway and then turn right alongside the A55 Expressway. Turn right at the T-junction with the B4545 and once over the Expressway, turn left into Lôn Spencer and follow it to **Valley** (35/4 miles).

Turn left towards Holyhead using the shared-use path alongside the A5 and follow it across the Stanley Embankment looking right to catch a glimpse

STAGE 5 – CAERNARFON TO HOLYHEAD

of the Skerries Lighthouse off the northwest corner of Anglesey. Once across the embankment follow the trail around **Penrhos Coastal Park** and into Penrhos Beach Road. After passing the hospital, turn right into Llanfawr Road and follow it to its end, passing over a mini-roundabout then turning right along a shared-use path towards the port and railway station. The route

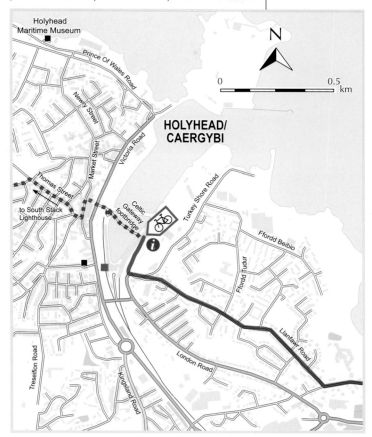

Parked up by the station and ferry port at Holyhead

officially ends at the Tourist Information Centre in the Stena Lines Building, which is next to the railway station at the entrance to Holyhead Port. However you may still find some NCR8 route signs that lead to a previous finish at Holyhead Maritime Museum on Prince of Wales Road. After cycling the length of Wales neither are heroic enough for me.

Alternative end at South Stack Lighthouse
Dismount and push your bike through the station concourse and over the Celtic Gateway footbridge. Turn left once you reach Market Street and walk through the pedestrian area then turn right into Thomas Street. After 350 metres, turn left into South Stack Road. After 3 miles turn right for the RSPB Centre, where there is a café, the lighthouse and some wonderful views across the Irish Sea. This has to be a better place to finish. ◀

Their red bill and legs make the noisy and playful choughs that live around South Stack easy to identify.

Looking down the steep path to South Stack Lighthouse

NORTH TO SOUTH

If you are riding north to south and you start out early you could easily get well beyond Caernarfon as this stage is remarkably flat.

APPENDIX A
Cycle shops

The following is a list of cycle shops on or near Lôn Las Cymru.

Abercynon
Sportouring
42 Margaret Street
Abercynon CF45 4RB
tel 01443 742 421
www.sportouring.co.uk

Abergavenny
Gateway Cycles
5 Brecon Road
Abergavenny NP7 5UH
tel 01873 858 519
www.gatewaycycles.co.uk

Bangor
Evolution Bikes
Cyttir Lane
Bangor LL57 4DA
tel 01248 355 770
www.evolution-bikes.co.uk

Brecon
Bi Ped Cycles
10 Ship Street
Brecon LD3 9AF
tel 01874 622 296
www.bipedcycles.co.uk

Builth Wells
Cycle-Tec
Bank Square
Builth Wells LD2 3BB
tel 01982 554 682
www.cycle-tec.co.uk

Caernarfon
Beics Menai Bikes
1 Cei Llechi
Caernarfon LL55 2PB
tel 01286 676 804

Cardiff
Bike Shed Wales
2B Merthyr Road, Tongwynlais
Cardiff CF15 7LF
tel 0292 081 1870
www.bikeshedwales.com

Cyclopaedia Ltd
116 Crwys Road
Cardiff CF24 4NR
tel 0292 037 7772
www.cyclopaedia.co.uk

Cygnus Cycles Mobile Repair
38 Doyle Avenue, Fairwater
Cardiff CF5 3HU
tel 07807 309 555
www.cygnuscycles.co.uk

Damian Harris Cycles
55 Merthyr Road
Cardiff CF14 1DD
tel 0292 0529 955
www.damianharriscycles.co.uk

Evans Cycles
Dumfries Place
Cardiff CF10 3FN
tel 0292 097 2700
www.evanscycles.com/store/cardiff

Outdoor Cycles
82 Pwllmelin Road
Cardiff CF5 2NH
tel 0292 056 4367
www.outdoorcycles.co.uk

plan2ride Bike Café
Rear of, 51 Merthyr Road
Tongwynlais
Cardiff CF15 7LG
tel 0292 081 0868
www.plan2ride.co.uk

Sunset Cycles
119–121 Woodville Road
Cardiff CF24 4DZ
tel 0292 039 0883
www.sunsetmtb.co.uk

Tredz Bikes
2 Penarth Road Retail Park
Penarth, Llandough
Cardiff CF11 8EF
tel 0292 070 2229
www.tredz.co.uk

Dolgellau
Dolgellau Cycles
The Old Furnace, Smithfield Street
Dolgellau LL40 1DF
tel 01341 423332
www.dolgellaucycles.co.uk

Hay-on-Wye
Drover Cycles
Forest Road
Hay-on-Wye HR3 5EH
tel 01497 822 419 or 07501 495 868
www.drovercycles.co.uk

Holyhead
Summit to Sea
Unit 10a, Penrhos Industrial Estate
Holyhead LL65 2UQ
tel 01407 740 963
www.summittosea.co.uk

Llanbedr
Snowdonia Cycles
Llanbedr LL45 2HN
tel 01341 241 916
www.snowdoniacycles.co.uk

Llandrindod Wells
Hubjub Cycling
Warwick House, High Street
Llandrindod Wells LD1 6AG
tel 01597 825 533
www.hubjub.co.uk

Merthyr Tydfil
EC Cycles
34 Heol S O Davies
Merthyr Tydfil CF48 1DR
tel 01685 382 700
www.eccycles.co.uk

Pontypridd
Halfords
Unit 4, Brown Lennox Retail Park
Ynysangharad Road
Pontypridd CF37 4DA
tel 01443 490 020
www.halfords.com

Porthmadog
K K Cycles
141 High Street
Porthmadog LL49 9HD
tel 01766 512 310

Rhayader
Elan Cyclery
West Street
Rhayader LD6 5AB
tel 01597 811 343
www.clivepowell-mtb.co.uk

Talybont-on-Usk
Bikes & Hikes
Talybont-on-Usk LD3 7YJ
tel 07909 968 135
www.bikesandhikes.co.uk

Treharris
DT Bicycles
Quakers Yard, Treharris
tel 01443 405 293
www.dtbicycles.co.uk

APPENDIX B
Accommodation

Hostels and bunkhouses

Barmouth
Bunkorama
Gwastad Agnes
Off Panorama Road
Barmouth
Gwynedd LL42 1DX
tel 01341 281 134/07738 467 196
www.bunkorama.co.uk

Bethesda
Caban Cysgu Gerlan Bunkhouse
Ffordd Gerlan
Gerlan, Bethesda
Bangor LL57 3ST
tel 01248 605 573/07464 676 753
www.cabancysgu-gerlan.co.uk

Brecon
The Star Bunkhouse
Brecon Road (A40)
Bwlch, Brecon
Powys LD3 7RQ
tel 01874 730 080/07341 906 937

Caernarfon
Totters
Plas Porth Yr Aur
2 High Street
Caernarfon
Gwynedd LL55 1RN
tel 01286 672 963/07979 830 470
www.totters.co.uk

Cardiff
River House Hostel
59 Fitzhamon Embankment
Riverside
Cardiff CF11 6AN
tel 0292 039 9810
www.riverhousebackpackers.com

Safehouse Hostel
3 Westgate Street
Cardiff CF10 1DD
tel 0292 037 2833
www.safehousehostel.co.uk

YHA Cardiff Central
East Tyndall Street
Cardiff CF10 4BB
tel 03453 719 311
www.yha.org.uk

Chepstow
Green Man Backpackers
13 Beaufort Square
Chepstow NP16 5EP
tel 01291 626 773
www.greenmanbackpackers.co.uk

Corris
Corris Hostel
Old School
Corris, Machynlleth
Powys SY20 9TQ
tel 01654 761 686
www.corrishostel.co.uk

Dolgellau
Hyb Bunkhouse
2–3 Heol y Bont (Bridge Street)
Dolgellau
Gwynedd LL40 1AU
tel 01341 421 755

Dylife
Y Star Inn Bunkhouse
Dylife
Llanbrynmair
Powys SY19 7BW
tel 01650 521 345
www.starinndylife.co.uk

Garndolbenmaen
Cwm Pennant Hostel
Golan
Garndolbenmaen
Gwynedd LL51 9AQ
tel 01766 530 888/01706 877 320
www.cwmpennanthostel.com

Glasbury
Woodlands Bunkhouse
Glasbury on Wye HR3 5LP
tel 01497 847 272
www.woodlandsoec.org

Holyhead
Anglesey Outdoor Centre
Porthdafarch Road
Holyhead LL65 2LP
tel 01407 769 351
www.angleseyoutdoors.com

Kings
YHA Kings
Penmaenpool
Dolgellau
Gwynedd LL40 1TB
tel 0345 371 9327
www.yha.org.uk

Llanidloes
Plasnewydd Bunkhouse
Gorn Road
Llanidloes
Powys SY18 6LA
tel 01686 412 431/07975 913 049
www.plasnewyddbunkhouse.co.uk

Llanellen
Middle Ninfa Bunkhouse
(2 miles up a steep lane above Llanfoist)
Llanellen
Abergavenny NP7 9LE
tel 01873 854 662
www.middleninfa.co.uk

Machynlleth
Toad Hall
Doll Street
Machynlleth
Powys SY20 8BH
tel 01654 700 597/07866 362 507

Newbridge-on-Wye
Llysdinam Field Centre
Newbridge-on-Wye
Llandrindod Wells
Powys LD1 6NB
tel 07514 358 330
www.llysdinamfieldcentre.co.uk

New Inn Bunkhouse
New Inn
Newbridge-on-Wye
Llandrindod Wells
Powys LD1 6HY
tel 01597 860 211
www.pigsfolly.co.uk

Pantygelli
Smithy's Bunkhouse
Lower House Farm
Pantygelli
Abergavenny NP7 7HR
tel 01873 853 432
www.smithysbunkhouse.co.uk

Rhayader
Beili Neuadd Bunkhouse
Beili Neuadd
Rhayader
Powys LD6 5NS
tel 01597 810 211
www.beilineuadd.co.uk

Rhoscolyn
Outdoor Alternative
Cerrig-yr-Adar
Rhoscolyn
Holyhead LL65 2NQ
tel 01407 860 469
www.outdooralternative.co.uk

St Briavels
YHA St Briavels Castle
St Briavels
Lydney
Gloucestershire GL15 6RG
tel 0345 371 9042
www.yha.org.uk

St Harmon
Mid Wales Bunkhouse
Woodhouse Farm
St Harmon
Rhayader LD6 5LY
tel 01597 870 081
www.bunkhousemidwales.co.uk

Talybont-on-Usk
The White Hart Inn & Bunkhouse
Talybont-on-Usk
Brecon LD3 7JD
tel 01874 676 227
www.whitehartinntalybont.co.uk

YHA Brecon Beacons Danywenallt
Talybont-on-Usk
Brecon
Powys LD3 7YS
tel 0345 371 9548
www.yha.org.uk

Waunfawr
Pentre Bach Bunkhouse
Pentre Bach
Waunfawr
Caernarfon
Gwynedd LL54 7AJ
tel 07798 733 939
www.pentrebachbunkhouse.co.uk

Campsites
The following organisations have websites that list campsites in Wales.

The Camping and Caravanning Club
www.campingandcaravanningclub.co.uk

Cool Camping
www.coolcamping.co.uk

UK Campsite
www.ukcampsite.co.uk

APPENDIX C
Useful contacts

The website www.visitwales.com is a useful resource.

Travel websites

Arriva Trains Wales
tel 0870 900 0773
www.arrivatrainswales.co.uk.

Great Western Railway
tel 0345 700 0125
www.gwr.com.

Irish Ferries
tel 08717 300 400
www.irishferries.co.uk.

National Rail
tel 08457 484 950
www.nationalrail.co.uk.

Stena Ferries
tel 0344 847 0008
www.stenaline.co.uk.

Traveline
tel 0871 200 2233
www.traveline.info
or www.traveline.cymru.

TrawsCymru
tel 0300 200 2233
www.trawscymru.info.

Virgin Trains
tel 0344 556 5650
www.virgintrains.co.uk.

Tourist information centres

Abergavenny
The Tithe Barn
Monk Street
Abergavenny NP7 5ND
tel 01873 858787

Barmouth (Seasonal)
The Old Library
Station Road
Barmouth
tel 01341 280 787

Brecon
Cattle Market
Brecon LD3 9DA
tel 01874 622 485

Builth Wells
The Groe
Builth Wells LD2 3BL
tel 01982 553 307

Caernarfon
Oriel Pendeitsh
Castle Ditch
Caernarfon LL55 1ES
tel 01286 672 232

Cardiff
The Old Library
9–11 The Hayes
Cardiff CF10 1AH
tel 0870 121 1258

Pier Head
Cardiff Bay CF10 5AL
tel 0292 046 3833

Chepstow
Bridge Street
Chepstow NP16 5EY
tel 01291 623 772

Corris (Seasonal)
Corris Craft Centre
Corris SY20 9RF
tel 01654 761 244

Dolgellau
Ty Meirion
Eldon Square
Dolgellau LL40 1LU
tel 01341 422 888

Harlech (Seasonal)
Llys Y Graig
High Street
Harlech LL46 2YA
tel 01766 780 658

Hay-on-Wye
Oxford Road
Hay-on-Wye HR3 5DG
tel 01497 820 144

Holyhead
Terminal 1
Stena Line Port
Holyhead LL65 1DQ
tel 01407 762 622

Llanfair Pwllgwyngyll
Station Site
Llanfair Pwllgwyngyll LL61 5UJ
tel 01248 713 177

Llanidloes
The Library
Mount Lane
Llanidloes SY18 6EY
tel 01686 412 855

Merthyr Tydfil
14a Glebeland Street
Merthyr Tydfil CF47 8AU
tel 01685 379 884

Pontypridd
Pontypridd Museum
Bridge Street
Pontypridd CF37 4PE
tel 01443 490 748

Porthmadog
High Street
Porthmadog LL49 9LD
tel 01766 512 981

Rhayader
The Leisure Centre
Rhayader LD6 5BU
tel 01982 553 307

APPENDIX D
What to take

Below is a checklist of things to take, together the typical weights of items that are carried.

Riding gear
- Helmet
- Balaclava or Buff®
- Cycling glasses
- Short-sleeved base layer
- Short-sleeved cycling jersey
- Arm warmers
- Cycling gloves
- Cycling shorts
- Leg warmers
- Socks
- Waterproof jacket (350gm)
- Waterproof over-trousers (300gm)
- Overshoes (150gm)

Leisurewear
- Long-sleeved T-shirt x 2 (150gm x 2)
- Underwear x 2 (100gm x 2)
- Micro-fleece top (420gm)
- Travel trousers (450gm)
- Socks x 2 (60gm x 2)
- Trainers/Crocs (600gm)
- Stuff bags (40gm x 2)

Additional leisurewear for cooler months
- Fleece jacket (550gm)
- Heavier travel trousers (550gm)

Tools and accessories
- Rear light (55gm)
- Front light (100gm)
- Pump (110gm)
- Multi-tool (120gm)
- Spoke key (17gm)
- Spare inner tube (120gm)
- Spare folding tyre or a 'boot' – section of old tyre for reinforcing splits and holes (350gm/50gm)
- Self-adhesive patches (20gm)
- Tyre levers (26gm)
- Powerlink (5gm)
- Set of cables (50gm)
- Latex gloves (3gm)
- Spare bolts x 2 (4gm)
- Cable ties x 2 (3gm)

Extras
- Toiletries (250gm)
- Travel towel (135gm)
- Sun cream (45gm)
- Lip salve (15gm)
- Wet wipes (50gm)
- Compact first aid kit (200gm)
- Map or GPS and charger (150gm)
- Guidebook (235gm)
- Itinerary (10gm)
- Pen (10gm)
- Compact camera (265gm)
- Phone and charger (270gm)
- Wallet/cards (100gm)

APPENDIX E
Welsh words and pronunciation

Common Welsh words found in place names

Welsh	English
aber	river mouth or estuary
afon	river
bach	small, little
bangor	monastery
bedd	grave
betws	chapel
blaenau	upland
bod	dwelling
bryn	hill
bwlch	pass, col, gap or saddle
bychan	small
cae	field
caer	fort or encampment
capel	chapel
carreg	stone
castell	castle
cefn	back/ridge
clas	church
coch	red
coed	wood
craig	crag
croes	cross
cwm	valley
din	hillfort

Welsh	English
dinas	large town or city
du	black
dŵr	water
dyffryn	valley
eglwys	church
fach	small
fawr	large
ffordd	road
ffridd	pasture
ffynnon	spring or well
gallt	wooded slope
garn	cairn
garth	hill
glan	riverbank or shore
glas	green, blue, grey or silver
glyn	valley
gwaun	bog
gwyn	white
hafod	summer dwelling
heol	road
hewl	road
isaf	lower
llan	church
llyn	lake
maen	stone
mawr	big
melin	mill

Welsh	English
moel	bare hill or mountain
morfa	marsh
mynydd	mountain
nant	stream/valley
newydd	new
pant	hollow/valley
pen	end
penrhyn	headland
pentref	village/hamlet
pont	bridge
porth	port or harbour
pwll	pool
rhaeadr	waterfall
rhiw	hill
rhos	moor
rhyd	ford
sir	shire
stryd	street
traeth	shore or beach
uchaf	upper

Description	Example
Ae, Ai and Au as the 'y' in my	*mae* (my), *craig* (crige)
Aw as the 'ow' in cow	*mawr* (mour), *fawr* (vour)
C always 'hard' as in cat	*cwm* (coomb), *Cymru* (Kumree)
Ch soft as in the Scottish loch	*fach* (vach)
Oe as the 'oy' in toy	*croes* (croys)
Dd as the 'th' in the or seethe	*bydd* (beethe); *carneddau* (carneth-eye)
F as the 'v' in five	*afon* (avon), *fawr* (vowr), *fach* (vach)
Ff as the 'f' in fight	*ffyrdd* (furth)
Ll is roughly the 'th' in theatre followed by 'l'	*llan* (thlan), *llyn* (thlin)
Ow as the 'ow' in cow	*Powys* (Pow-iss)
Rh sounds as if the h comes before the r	*rhyd* (hrid)
U as the 'ee' in reel	*Cymru* (Kum-ree)
W as the 'oo' in zoo	*cwm* (koom), *bwlch* (boolch)
Wy as the 'wi' in with	*Wyddfa* (with-va)
Wy as the 'ue' in clue	*Clwyd* (Cloohwid)

A simple guide to Welsh pronunciation

R is always pronounced and always rolled. Do not pronounce AR, ER, IR, OR, UR or YR as they are in English but just pronounce the short vowel with a rolling R after it so ER will sounds a bit like the English air; IR, UR, YR as final syllables all sound like the English deer; and YR as non-final syllables like the English fur.

Below is a simple guide to pronouncing consonants, vowels and the more common combinations found in Welsh place names.

APPENDIX F

Selected additional reading

Cardiff and the Marquesses of Bute, John Davies (University of Wales Press, 2011)

Dr Beeching's Axe 50 Years On, Julian Holland (David & Charles 2013)

The Grand Designer: Third Marquess of Bute, Rosemary Hannah (Birlinn, 2013)

A History of Wales, John Davies (Penguin, 2007)

Iconic Cycling Trails in Wales, Phil Horsley (Gwasg Carreg Gwalch, 2017)

Merthyr, the Crucible of Modern Wales, Joe England (Parthian Books 2017)

Owain Glyn Dŵr Prince of Wales, RR Davies (Y Lolfa, 2011)

The Rough Guide to Wales, Tim Burford (Rough Guides, 2018)

The Story of Wales, Jon Gower (BBC, 2013)

The Welsh Cake Cookbook, Gill Davies (Graffeg, 2016)

NOTES

DOWNLOAD THE ROUTES
IN GPX FORMAT

All the routes in this guide are available for download as GPX files from:

www.cicerone.co.uk/987/GPX

You should be able to load them into most formats of mobile device, whether GPS or smartphone.

When you go to this link, you will be asked for your email address and where you purchased the guide, and have the option to subscribe to the Cicerone e-newsletter.

www.cicerone.co.uk

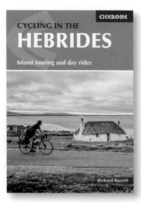
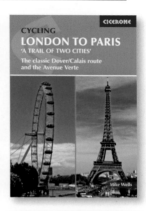
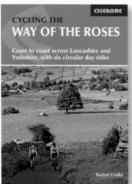
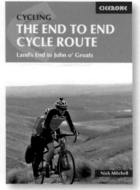

Walking – Trekking – Mountaineering – Climbing – Cycling

Over 40 years, Cicerone have built up an outstanding collection of over 300 guides, inspiring all sorts of amazing adventures.

Every guide comes from extensive exploration and research by our expert authors, all with a passion for their subjects. They are frequently praised, endorsed and used by clubs, instructors and outdoor organisations.

All our titles can now be bought as **e-books**, **ePubs** and **Kindle** files and we also have an online magazine – **Cicerone Extra** – with features to help cyclists, climbers, walkers and trekkers choose their next adventure, at home or abroad.

Our website shows any **new information** we've had in since a book was published. Please do let us know if you find anything has changed, so that we can publish the latest details. On our **website** you'll also find great ideas and lots of detailed information about what's inside every guide and you can buy **individual routes** from many of them online.

It's easy to keep in touch with what's going on at Cicerone by getting our monthly **free e-newsletter**, which is full of offers, competitions, up-to-date information and topical articles. You can subscribe on our home page and also follow us on **Facebook** and **Twitter** or dip into our **blog**.

Cicerone – the very best guides for exploring the world.

CICERONE

Juniper House, Murley Moss, Oxenholme Road, Kendal, Cumbria LA9 7RL
Tel: 015395 62069 info@cicerone.co.uk
www.cicerone.co.uk